Henry William Bunbury, Richard Cobbold

Geoffery Gambado

A simple remedy for hypochondriacism and melancholy splenetic humours

Henry William Bunbury, Richard Cobbold

Geoffery Gambado
A simple remedy for hypochondriacism and melancholy splenetic humours

ISBN/EAN: 9783337283100

Printed in Europe, USA, Canada, Australia, Japan

Cover: Foto ©Suzi / pixelio.de

More available books at **www.hansebooks.com**

Geoffery Gambado;

OR,

A SIMPLE REMEDY FOR

HYPOCHONDRIACISM

AND

MELANCHOLY SPLENETIC HUMOURS.

BY A HUMORIST PHYSICIAN.

Honi soit qui mal y pense.

PRINTED, FOR THE AUTHOR, BY DEAN & SON, LUDGATE HILL, LONDON.

Preface.

SOME years ago, sixteen original sketches by Henry
Bunbury, Esq. were given to the Author of this
Book. This celebrated sketcher and caricaturist
was a gentleman well known in the county of Suffolk for
his public and private virtues, as well as for his superior
talents. He was a lineal descendant of the Rev. Sir
William Bunbury, whose baronetcy was created in 1681.
Of a cheerful and lively temper, he sought to infuse
the same spirit through all ranks of society. If we
mistake not, his son became Sir Henry Bunbury, and
represented the county of Suffolk, as his uncle, Sir
Thomas Charles Bunbury, had done before him.

His descendants still occupy the mansion and estates in

Suffolk, where they have been, and are still, the great benefactors to the poor, and the parish of Great Barton near Bury St. Edmund's.

But we have to speak more particularly of Henry Bunbury, Esq. and his talents. To this day, his accurate delineations of the political and social customs of the age he lived in, and of the characters who came under his observation, are remarkable for their truthful force. It is very seldom that men of high life and good education, possess the artistic power of graphic delineation: at least, we have but few amateur delineators who can stand the test of the invidious sneers and jeers of those empty possessors of wealth and station, who consider themselves degraded even by the acquaintance of an artist, a poet, or a literary character. Now, if a man is not a degraded man, but lives himself after the law of God, he need never mind the scoffs or ridicule of any man; but may say, as Henry Bunbury did to those who ridiculed him,—" Evil be to him who evil thinks."

In the Sketches contained in this work, the difficulty

was to make out what kind of story they told ; for though some persons might see in them nothing more than ridicule upon the *Annals of Complete Horsemanship*, yet those who knew the man, and knew the disposition he always entertained, namely, a desire to do evil to no man, but good to all, thought that his intention was to cure some over-sensitive minds of morbid and melancholy feelings, which ought not, unreasonably and unseasonably, to overwhelm them, and destroy their energies.

It was not that he ridiculed real affliction, or ever, in any one of his drawings, sought to give a pang to the real mourner ; but he really loved a cheerful disposition ; and could not bear that man should be afflicting himself with imaginary diseases, when a little self-exertion, or diversion, would restore his right tone of bodily health, and be the means of doing him good.

We have adopted these views of our celebrated talented Suffolk gentleman, and have endeavoured to turn his pictures to this profitable account. They represent horses, and costume of fashion or fiction, long since exploded; but they represented real persons, whom he knew, and many were reckoned inimitable likenesses. Caricature is itself a species of broad, or excessive resemblance of fact; let it be represented by Shakspeare's Falstaff,—Hogarth's Marriage a la Mode,—Dickens' Pickwick Papers,—Macaulay's Stories of Historical Persons, (introduced into his popular History of England),—or of Punch,—or of that greatest of all powerful pencil delineators of character, George Cruikshank. We leave out the popular novelists, or poets, who have written funny as well as serious things;—all, more or less, have taken advantage of caricature skill, to prove their acquaintance with the ridiculous.

Cowper is generally looked upon as a serious poet, yet he wrote "Johnny Gilpin." But we will make no more excuses for our present work. We will only add that it was originally conceived for a charitable purpose, and is now made use of as such.

The Author of the Illustrations has long since departed this mortal life; and the Author of the Narrative, not seeking the reputation of his own name, does not give it to the world; but, apologizing for his interpretation of the sketches, desires only to do good. If any should be entertained, and will kindly send any mark of their favour to the Publisher, for the Author, the word of a Gentleman is given, that, whatever it may be, it shall be strictly devoted to public good.

THE FRONTISPIECE.

" R EADER ! did you ever see an angel on horseback ?'
" No !" No more did I, that I know of ! We read
of one in (II. Maccabeus, c. 3) ; but then he was clad in
armour of gold, and rode a most powerful animal, who
smote with his forelegs the avaricious Heliodorus. But
here we see a very different representation, both as to
horse and rider, and engaged in trumpeting forth the
praises of the celebrated

DOCTOR GAMBADO.

" Gambado ! Sempre viva ! Encora ! Encora !" In fact, it
is termed "The Apotheosis of Geoffery Gambado, Esq.
M. D. F. R. S."

Now this angel might be a daughter of Doctor Gambado's, or she might be his scullery-maid. She is represented on a horse, which, instead of being a winged
Pegasus, stands well upon his pegs, and seems to have

SEMPRE VIVA ENCORA ENCOR

GAMBADO

GAMBADO

H Bunbury Esq: Inv.

THE APOTHEOSIS OF GEOFFERY GAMBADO. MD

lent his wings to the damsel herself, to bear both himself and her "in nubibus." She holds a medallion of the Doctor, a striking portrait, in her right hand; and in her left, the celebrated brazen trumpet of Fame; and, no doubt, whether his angelic daughter or his faithful domestic, she was one who knew so well the admirable worth of the good physician, that she simply means to say,—" May the cheerful spirit of such good men as Doctor Gambado live for ever, and drive out of all splenetic patients, the tormenting stings of the Blue Devils."

If he can do this, his canonization will indeed be immortal, though it be trumpeted forth by so humble an instrument as the angel we here see represented on a wooden horse.

Reader, the humblest instrument in the world may, in the hand of wisdom, be used as an angel for your own good. The poor fellow who lifts you up from the ground, should you happen to fall, may be the helping hand provided you. The messenger who finds you in suffering, and sends the doctor to your relief, may be the unknown angel for your deliverance.

A poor boy, or a poor girl, who snatches you, in your infant days, from the peril of a pond, may be used as an angel for your welfare.

Do not always expect to see angels in golden armour for your deliverance; though the generous and charitably-good Samaritan, the friend in need, may be the friend indeed at the hour you most require him,— only be humble, only be thankful, and even this poor picture may be a message of comfort to your spirit;   for

> "Reproof is better than a great man's gold;
> And he is good who loves a thing well told:
> Then 'evil be to him who thinks the same,'
> And would destroy Gambado's honest fame."

Henry Bunbury Esq.ʳ inv.   R.C

CHAPTER I.

Gambado himself seeing the world in a six miles' tour.

IT is time we should speak something of this celebrated person, and account for his present position and appearance. He is very unlike any modern physician. A hundred years ago, however, we have no doubt that such was a fac-simile of this noble specimen of an equestrian medical proficient. It is a hundred years ago since the original sketch of him was made, which we have endeavoured to copy. We have to account for finding him in such a position. First, Who was he? What was he? Where did he live? What did he do? And how came he into notice at all?

Most men are born somewhere! and except they become noted for something they have done, it is very seldom that any inquiry is made about them at all. Neither the place of their birth, nor the locale of their ·

fame, or name, or habitation, of their death, or marriage, is made of any moment whatsoever.

Alas! those who are most ambitious of fame, seldom get it whilst they live; and very few, ever, as literary men, are exalted to a title, like Lord Macaulay; whilst those often feel they are praised for what they own they do not deserve, are more humbled by their reputation, than they are exalted.

It was said to Gambado, in the day of his greatest reputation, "We will certainly have you in Westminster Abbey?"

"Thank you, my dear fellow," was his reply; "I would rather eat a mutton chop with you at the Mermaid Tavern, in the street I was born in, than lie along with John Milton, (who was born in the next street to mine), or with any of those worthies, Shakspeare, Raleigh, or Ben Jonson; who can no longer eat a mutton chop with us at their old Tavern:

> "'I seek no fame, I want no name,
> My bread in Bread-street is:
> Gambado has sufficient fame;
> This is sufficient bliss!'"

He was born in Bread-street, in Cheapside: and in the first year of the reign of George the Third, A.D. 1760, he was in full practice and celebrity, and could not be less than forty years of age. As to whom he married, and what became of his wife and one lovely daughter, we know not. They appear conspicuously only in the last pages of this narrative, and were evidently in the enjoyment of all their great master's reputation, as well as in the keeping up with him in partaking of his own favourite panacea for all complaints, viz.—the riding on horseback.

But how came he to take up this exercise? to stick to it? and to recommend it as he did upon every occasion? Simply, as he told every one, because he found in it a sure and certain remedy for that dreadful nervous disease, commonly known by the name of the "Blue Devils."

Few things gave greater offence in that day to the Faculty, than Dr. Gambado's system of practice. He prescribed very little, if any, medicine : he certainly gave none to those whom he considered did not require it. He knew the power of a strong mind over a weak body, and what too great fatigue of either would produce. He knew well, moreover, the danger of entertaining too much imagination upon any complaint. He was acknowledged by all to be well versed in the physical construction of the human frame ; and especially of that most complicated portion, the nervous system, to which he had paid such scientific attention that his *Vocabulary of Nervous*

Constitutions was his great work, that won for him much scientific fame, and got him the honour of being elected F. R. S. before he attained such practical success as made his fortune.   He did make a great fortune; and he was honest enough to confess that he owed the enjoyment of it, if not the possession of it, entirely to a Horse-dealer.

He was, himself, at one period of his life, so completely prostrated in his own nervous system, that, from the crown of his head to the sole of his feet, he was completely unstrung.   He was constantly in the habit of going to church with his wife and daughter, at St. Stephen's, Walbrook, one of Sir Christopher Wren's most beautiful specimens of architecture; but in his depression he shunned the company of those he loved best on earth, and almost forsook his God and his duty, imagining himself totally forsaken of Him and every friend.   He had no pleasure in any thing.   His very profession was a burthen to him, and night and day he did nothing but mope. What would have become of him, his wife and daughter, his practice, his home, and his society, had he not, as he used to say, met with an angel, in the shape of a horse-dealer?

He was strolling, one evening, in a very melancholy mood, down Friday-street, not far from his own home, as he passed by the livery stables of John *Tattsall*, as the name was then spelt. John knew the doctor, and capped him with " A beautiful evening, sir."

The Doctor stopped, and looking very woefully in his · face, said, " Yes, John, very beautiful to those who are well."

" Yes sir, and to those who are sick, too; and I wish they could enjoy it."

" John, I am very ill myself, and have been so for some time. I shall not write many more prescriptions !"

" I hope you won't, sir ; I hope you won't."

" Why so, John ? why so ?"

" Because you gentlemen prescribe so much advice, and so seldom follow any good advice yourselves, that you are sure to die sooner than any other men. You all know too much about other people, and very little about yourselves."

" You are a blunt fellow, John ; but I do not like you the less for that. You once consulted me, did you not ?"

" Yes, sir, and you told me the truth ; and I liked you all the better for it. You told me plainly there was nothing the matter with me. ' Go home,' you said, ' drink a glass of cold water just before you get into bed ; and if that do not do you more good than any medicine I can give you, then come to me again, bring me another guinea, and I will give you the same advice.' I did as

you advised, and it was the best cold water cure that ever
was effected : I have never been ill since. But, Doctor,
I have heard that you are out of sorts. One good turn
deserves another, and if you will follow my advice, only
for one week, you shall be a different man to what you
now are. You shall soon earn your hundreds ; and only
give me one guinea in the hundred, and you will make my
fortune and your own too."

"What is your advice? I will agree to the terms."

"Well, Doctor, let me tell you the truth. You have
done too much,—studied too much,—wrote too much,—
thought too much,—and have overdone everything, and
now find you can do nothing. You are fast sinking into
that lapsed condition in which you will soon become an
inmate of Bedlam, if you go on as you have done of late.
You grow enormously fat, and are getting like the pig in
my stye, and will soon be snoring, snoring, snoring, all
day long, a plague to yourself and every-one else. If you
do not follow my advice, you will be a dead man before
you ever eat another Christmas turkey."

"What is it, John?"

"Ride out six miles on horseback, every morning at six
o'clock,—and six miles back again,—and that for six days ;
and if, at the end of that time, your lethargic state is not
improved, then say, John Tattsall is a good-for-nothing
humbug, and deserves to be well horsewhipped."

" But, John, I never rode on horseback in my life:
never was in the habit of it. I do not think I ever could."

" *Master, you must try, if you would not die.*"

Now the Doctor did not like the thought of dying,
though he had seen so much of it when it touched others.
A strange kind of nervous sensation ran through him,—
not through his veins, for he was one who wrote against
"vasicular nerves,"—but it ran through his system, as he
thought of John's words, " *Master, you must try, if you would
not die.*"

" Well John,—I will try,—but you must teach me ! "

" Come, master, that's right ; nothing like trying to amend
our ways before its too late," as good Doctor Cassock
said. So a good beginning, well followed up, and, barring
accident, I see no reason, Doctor, why you should not
live for forty years longer. You know well, that a man
overworked, like any other animal, is soon worn out;
and a man who does no work, very soon dies. Just come
and look at a nice little Norway cob I have in my
stable ; quiet and gentle as a lamb. A very few turns
down my ride, will give you a seat in the saddle, and you
shall be again a happy man."

The Doctor got into the saddle that very evening ; and
nobody saw him, but John ; and if the stable boys peeped
out and smiled, they got a little back-handed tip with

their master's whip, and were glad to hide their diminished
heads in the straw.   He went home a little more cheerful ; played a game of backgammon with his wife, and
kissed the cheek of his only child Kate, and seemed a
little better.   To the surprise of his family, he ordered
hot water into his dressing-room, at half-past five in the
morning ; and, of course, it was thought he was going to
take a journey.   He did so ; but when he went out, he
said, " I shall breakfast at half-past eight o'clock."

So the Doctor took a six miles' tour every morning, for
six days.   He improved daily; and though he rode very
awkwardly at first, holding on by the reins, and keeping
his brow bent and his eye intent upon the Norway Cob's
ears, his daily exercise did him a world of good ; and
before the week was out, he began to find himself a
different creature.   At the end of the week, he gave John
Tattsall fifty guineas for the Cob; and a friendship,
founded upon mutual accommodation, subsisted between
them, to the day of their deaths.

So was a horse-dealer made an angel or messenger of
health to the mournful spirit or unstrung nerves of
Doctor Geoffery Gambado.   He had the honesty to own
it.   The Doctor perfectly recovered his right mind and
bodily health ; and, like a wise man, who well knows
that the same thing which does him good may do others

the same, he took more patients to John Tattsall's livery stables than he ever sent to the sea side, to Madeira, to Buxton, or to Margate, Ramsgate, or any other gate whatsoever. John kept horses to suit all comers and all customers, and found Doctor Gambado the most grateful of all, because he always owned that, beneath a good Providence, he did him great good.

The Doctor's fame rapidly increased with the increase of his health. He soon became the very first Physician in nervous complaints. He knew the cause of nervous degeneracy,—no man better. He recommended *Tattsall* to all such patients as he found likely to be benefitted by him ;' and they were not a few. His letters, if they could be collected, would be found as direct to the point as the Wellington despatches.

"John,—I want just such a horse as cured me, to cure an old fool like myself.

Yours, &c.—GAMBADO."

John, like a well-tutored chemist, understood the peculiar character of the Doctor's prescriptions, which, unlike a quack's, were generally written in a plain, legible hand, without any *ad captandum* humbug. John had horses from twenty-five to five-hundred guineas each.

But as the Doctor's fame increased, so, it might be truly

said, the follies of "hypochondriacism" began to be
exposed. People, and especially those of the Great Faculty,
were jealous of the Doctor's reputation.   It is always
a sign of a little mind to be envious, or jealous of another
man's celebrity. Take it for granted, when you hear a
man speak slightingly of another, set that man down, who-
ever he is, for a conceited ass himself, or an ambitious, if
not an envious and wretched man.   Better speak nothing,
than speak evil of another ; better correct an evil thought,
than have to repent of an evil act.   Some called the
Doctor a mere visionary practitioner, or a mere veterinary
surgeon, or a quack, or anything else.   But he kept on
his course.   We have selected a few of the strange cases
that came before him a hundred years ago.

> What changes in a hundred years !
>   What fashions, and what dress !
> What troubles, woes, and bloody tears,
>   The world must now confess !
>
> Avoid them all,—seck peace and love,—
>   Be humble and be wise ;
> May this poor book some comfort prove
>   To friends, and enemies.

Henry Bunbury Esqr. inv

CHAPTER II.

A Brother Patient.—How to make the least use of a Horse.

IT was not long before the Doctor received a visit from an old friend; one, who had, in younger days, been a student in the same school, and entered into practice about the same time. The servant introduced Doctor Bull,—yes, Doctor John Bull, or, more properly styled, John Bull, Esq. M.D.—but not F.R.S. No, Doctor Bull had been more ambitious of practising, than of obtaining an empty name. He was a steady, well-to-do little man, and never lost a patient from any want of good manners or attention. He had certainly given much thought to the subject of *Hydrophobia*, and was considered no mean authority in the treatment of cases pronounced very malignant; but he by no means confined his abilities to that one branch of human misfortune.

He advised well with the Surgeons, and, generally, approved their treatment; but suggested frequently that judicious change which the nature of the case required. This he did in so gentlemanly and considerate a manner, that he was sure to be consulted by the very next patient of the same Surgeon.

In this way, he made many friends, lost very few, and found himself in the most affluent circumstances from very extensive practice. But, somehow, he overworked himself, and got into a very irritable, and at the same time desponding, tone. Prosperity, tries men very often more severely than adversity.

The Doctor, as long as he had his way to make in the world, was more attentive to others, and thought less about his own ails than he did about others. Now that he had accumulated money, he began to think of investments, and how he should place to the best account his accumulations.

He also thought a little more of style, equipage, choice society, and innumerable things, to which his life had been hitherto a stranger. He began to think and to care more about himself, than he did about any body else. He became of some consequence in his neighbourhood, and expected every one to bow to him, and to treat him as a *monied man.* In short, from a pure philanthropist, he became almost a misanthrope.

He began to torment himself about every thing and

every body. Nothing pleased him,—his wife and children disturbed him,—he was downright cross to them. And the same man, who once never came into his house without a cheerful smile for every one in it, now took no notice of anyone, except it were to find fault, and to let out words which in his sober senses he would be shocked to hear any other person make use of.

" My dear, I am sure you are not well," said Mrs. Bull, to him one day, " I am sure you are not well."

" I could have told you that," was the reply.

" Do take a little change."

" Pish! change! what change? I am changing, and shall soon make some great change, if things go on as they do in this house?

" Is anything wrong, my dear? "

" Yes, everything is wrong,—nothing is right,—all things are out of order,—and everything wants a change."

" Well, my dear, I think, if we took a house for three months at Brighton, it would do us all good."

" What good, madam? And who is to pay for it? What will become of my patients? and how am I to support my family? Brighton indeed! No, no! If I cannot be better without going to Brighton, I had better decline at home! Who is to look after my patients?"

" Why, there is Doctor Goodfellow, who I am sure you admire.   He will attend any of your patients for you. Do, my dear, have a little compassion upon yourself."

" And, I suppose, upon you to ; upon Kitty as well; upon Mary, Patty, and little Johnny; servants and all,—Heigh ! "

" If you please, my dear, even so, for you have not had much compassion upon any of us lately; and a change towards us all would be very agreeable."

A good wife has nothing to fear, and especially when she knows that she so loves her husband as to desire his health above all things else, whether of body, mind, or spirit.   If a wife may not expostulate with her husband, who may?   And notwithstanding all his perverseness, she had her own way with him, because she felt it was right.

To Brighton they all went; but the fancy had taken too strong hold upon Doctor Bull, to let him rest.   He worried himself because he was away from London,—he worried himself about the state of his patients,—the price of stocks,—the state of his own pulse, tongue, eyes, and lungs,—till he could endure himself no longer.

" I must go and see my old friend Gambado; I know he is a clever man, and has paid great attention to the nervous system, I must go and see him.   He ordered his chariot, and drove to Bread-street; sent in his card, and was very soon shaking hands with his quondam friend Doctor Gambado.

" Bull, I am glad to see you! You are not come to consult me professionally about yourself, I hope ? "

" I am, though, and about nobody else."

" Then what's the matter with you ? "

" Dispeptic."

" Is that all ? " " No ! Choleric ? " " Is that all ?" " No." " What is the matter ? out with it."

" To tell you the truth, Geoffery, I hardly know how to describe myself to you ? You never were afflicted in the same way."

" How do you know that ? "

" I am sure of it. You never were tormented morning, noon, and night. You never hated your profession, as I do mine. You never felt that you killed a great many more than you cured ! You never loathed the sight of your wife and children, your house, servants, food, bed, board and lodging. In short, I am a regular monster to myself, and shall soon be good for nothing ! Did you ever feel so, my friend ? "

" Yes, and ten thousand times worse than all you have described."

" My dear friend, it is impossible."

"You may think it so,—and I certainly thought, once, exactly as you do now,—I can therefore make allowances for you. I tell you, no one ever appears so bad to any man, as the afflicted man does to himself. He would soon be better if he could once see others worse than himself, or as bad as himself, and wish, heartily wish, to see them cured. I tell you, such was my case—even worse than yours,—and I can cure you."

"Will you, my dear friend? will you?"

"Yes, will I; and as we never take fees of the faculty, therefore, I will cure you for nothing. I do not say, with nothing.—No. Will you follow my advice?"

"Yes, assuredly. What is it?"

"Ride on horseback."

"I never did so since I was a boy."

"Nor did I, till I tried."

"But did that cure you?"

"Yes, it did; and will cure you also."

"How long did you ride before you felt better?"

"Not an hour."

"How long before you were well again?"

"Six days; six miles out, every day; six miles home; and in six days all those morbid secretions went away from my brain, and I became as I am, a cheerful and happy man."

" But how shall I manage? I must begin *de novo*. I must learn, and I must get a horse that will just move as I want him, slow and sure; either a walk, or a gentle canter; one that does not mind the whip; and I dare not ride one with a spur."

" My dear fellow, I have a friend who served me with a horse just as I wanted it; and I have no doubt he can serve you just as well. I will write him a note, and you shall take it to him yourself."

Accordingly, the Doctor wrote him one of his laconic Epistles.

" DEAR TATT.—Mount my brother Doctor; give him a stiff-one, and one that will require a little exercise of the *deltoides* of the right arm. He can pay. Suit him well.

Your's, faithfully,—GEOFFERY GAMBADO."
" Mr. John Tattsall."

Now the celebrated Doctor Bull had as good a pair of carriage horses as any Squire Bull in England. Tatt. certainly mounted him on one " that he could not " *make the least of.* He was quiet enough, stiff enough, slow enough, steady enough; he did not mind the whip, for the Doctor might cut him over the head, neck, ears, and under the flank, and anywhere, and everywhere else; but the beast had no animation. The more he punished him, he only went the surest way to show to the world, *How to make the least of a horse.*

A few days after his *horse exercise*, he called on his friend Doctor Gambado, and said, " Doctor, I am certainly better; but I believe I should have been quite as well, if I had mounted a saddler's wooden horse, and tried to make him go, as I am in trying to make your friend Tattsall's horse go. I could not have believed it possible that any beast could bear without motion such a dose of whip-cord as I have administered to him."

"You asked for one that would bear the whip : did you not?"

" Yes, and one that was steady, did not shy, and would go very gently even a slow pace; but this horse has no pace at all."

" Well, my good old friend, I am glad you are better; that's a great point. I have no doubt, none in the world, that if you could mount Master Johnny's rocking-horse, and would do so, and have a good game of romps with your boy, it would do you as much good as showing to the world *how to make the least of a horse,*" by kicking, flogging, checking his rein, and trying to persuade him to go on.

" But if you will only walk down with me to John

Tattsall's stables, I have no doubt you will quickly learn a lesson of equestrian management that shall soon set you right with the public, and most especially with yourself. You have learnt nothing but how to make the least of a horse. Let my servant take your horse back; and if John Tattsall do not soon show you *how to make the most of a horse,* then do not pay him either for his horse or for his pains ; but set all down to my account. Be seated, my dear fellow, whilst I send your horse back with a note. The Doctor wrote—

" DEAR JOHN,—My brother Bull wants to learn how to make the most of a horse. We will be with you in the course of an hour.

Ever yours,—GEOFFERY GAMBADO."
"Mr. John Tattsall."

The brothers M.D. sat down to an hour's chat upon politics, stocks, dividends, and philosophy ; and at the end of one hour were seen wending their way arm-in-arm to the celebrated *Livery Stables* of John Tattsall, whither we will follow them, just to see if we can behold a contrast.

Far we need not go, to see
What makes a contrariety.

CHAPTER III.

How to make the most of a horse.

ARRIVED at the stables, it was not long before Doctor Gambado introduced his brother and friend Doctor Bull to the noted personage of his day, John Tattsall. Is the name of Tattsall, as it used to be called, corrupted, from a hundred years ago, now to that of Tattersall? We do not know the gentleman's dealer, auctioner, or horse agent of the latter name; but if he be the descendant of the great John Tattsall, we only hope he is as good a man as his ancestor. A better in his line could never be. It requires a knowledge of a man's craft, to say whether he is a good or bad workmen at it. We have very little knowledge of horse-dealers' craft, but their profits must be very great,—when the licence is set so high as five and twenty pounds, before they can practise the economy of horse-dealing. A hundred years ago, and the tax was not so high.

"This, John, is my friend, Doctor Bull, whom I recommended to your notice to find him a horse in every respect quiet, without vice, and gentle,—one who would bear the whip and not kick."

"Can the gentleman say I have not suited him?"

"I do not say I am not suited, but I had almost as soon be nonsuited in a case of law, as be suited with so inactive a beast to ride."

"Ah! sir, you speak like a tyro concerning the law. If you were once *nonsuited,* and had all the costs to pay in an action-at-law, believe me, sir, the being *non suited* in a horse which had no action, would be greatly preferable to all the success of a case-at-law, though you were told at the time that you got off cheap, after paying £150. Look, sir, at that cheque:

"Please to pay to Messrs. Runner and Co. the sum of three hundred pounds, on account of transfer of property, to the account of

Yours, faithfully,

CURRY AND POWDER."

How would you like that?"

"I should not like it at all; but there are many things in law and horse-dealing, which the least said about them the soonest ended."

"And also in other things as well. But bring out the gentleman's chestnut horse, Sam."

This was spoken to the groom, who knew his master's voice, and presently brought forth the very self-same horse, sent back to the stables one hour previously, as inactive: now behold him as lively as a lark.

What had been done to him, those acquainted with the art of renovation could alone tell; but here was a contrariety without going far to find it. The legs had been trimmed, the tail set up; and when the said John Tattsall mounted him, the man and horse seemed to become each other. John was a true specimen of an upright horse-dealer, a hundred years ago. Coat was buttoned up, hat almost as conspicuous as the Field Marshal's on the day of a grand review. Stick under his arm, easy seat in his saddle, long spurs, short breeches, brown periwig, and such a contour of character, that when he touched him with the spur, the fiery-eyed charger set off at a Hyde Park canter, to the delight of his learned spectators.

No one could be more pleased than Doctor Bull. "Aye! that is the way to make the most of a horse." Could I but make as much of him as that, he would be, of all creatures, the very one to set me up again? That will do, Mr. Tattsall, that will do. You have given me a good lesson how to make the most of a horse."

"Then, sir, you must let me make the most of him alone. One hundred guineas, is his price; and this is my advice to you, never take this horse out of his stable without giving him a good brush-up first. And never get on to his back, without a pair of spurs on your feet; and you will find him as pleasant a little park horse as any gentleman could ever wish to ride."

The money was paid, and *John Tattsall made the most of him.* But Doctor Bull made all that he expected out of him; namely, a restoration from a fit of Hypochondriacism into which he never after relapsed; but owed his cure to the honest advice of Geoffery Gambado, Esq. M.D. F.R.S.

" The simplest remedy, is mostly sure;
'T will never kill; but almost always cure."

D

CHAPTER IV.

Love and Wind.

THE Doctor sat in his easy chair reading, as was his custom, the Morning Star. That paper was then, what the Times is now. The Star had the ascendant, but the Times outshone the Star. There is a season for every thing under the sun ; and two more variable things under the sun can scarcely be mentioned, than the two at the head of this chapter. No two, however, will, with all their variations of calm and storm, be more lasting than these will be found to be, to the end of time. The Times, and all connected therewith, will have an end. Love knows no end. The Times may change as often as the winds, but it will be an ill wind indeed that blows nobody any good.

But the Doctor was interrupted in his perusal of his paper by the entrance of his factotum of a servant man, Samuel Footman. Sam was steward and porter, and waiting man and butler, and a very worthy fellow too,

Henry Bunbury Esq. inv.

for in every thing he was trustworthy, the best quality any man on earth, or woman either, can possess. Sam presented a card, saying the gentleman's carriage was at the door, and he wanted to know if you were at home. The Doctor looked at it. "Show Sir Nicholas Skinner up, Sam."

There entered into the Doctor's presence the most melancholy half-starved spectacle of humanity that he had ever seen ; almost a walking skeleton,— tall, thin, gaunt, and cadaverous,—melancholy in the extreme, eyes sunken, lips drawn down so as almost to form a semi-circular mouth ; long, lank, thin light hair ; a rough frill of the most delicate white round his neck. His coat was buttoned round a waist as thin as any woman's could be, and his eyes were sharp, black, piercing, and poetical. "Pray, Sir Nicholas, be seated," said the good Doctor, "you seem fatigued."

"I am so indeed ! I have travelled all night, with post horses, all the way from Salisbury, on purpose to consult you, Doctor ; for I have heard that you are famous in the cure of all nervous debility, and I verily believe every nerve in my frame is shattered. How I have sustained the journey and its fatigue I can scarcely tell; but I suppose it was the hope of living for another, that gave me support."

Here the gentleman gave so long and so deep a drawn

sigh, that it convinced the Doctor at once, that this was
one of those cases of hopeless malady, *disappointed love;*
which nothing but one thing could either kill or cure,
namely *matrimony.* The Doctor very seldom ventured to
recommend this universal specific for one thing or the
other. It was not exactly in his line.

"Let me feel your pulse." This he did; he also
sounded his lungs, looked into his eyes, and listened to
the pulsation of his heart.

"Ah!" he said, "there is a little irregularity there. All
is not exactly right in the region of the heart. It appears
to me to be slightly disorganized."

"Not slightly, I assure you, Doctor; not slightly; I
am affraid, severely!" And this was spoken so very
solemnly, that the Doctor, though he felt disposed to smile,
could not find it in his heart to treat the case slightingly.

"Have you had any advice at Salisbury? Have you
been under any medical treatment?"

"O yes; yes, sir; Doctor Crosse has attended me for
the last twelve months. He treats my case as one of
decline, or consumption. I was once as robust as you
are, Doctor; but I have wasted away to a shadow within
the space of one year."

"Pray, sir, are you a married man?"

"No-o-o! No-o-o! Not exactly that, but I am an engaged man. They do tell me, I must be in better health

before 1 marry; and that makes me very, very anxious to get better. They will scarcely allow the slightest breath of wind to blow upon me; no air, no exercise, no window down, no curtain undrawn, one even temperature,—and nothing must disturb me. Oh! Doctor, I fear I never shall marry. My intended is very careful over me. She has come up, all the way to town with me, as my nurse; and is now in my carriage at your door."

"Dear me, sir! why did you not tell me this before? It is actually necessary that I should see your good nurse, and have a few minutes' conversation with her. I am so glad you have brought her; it gives me the greatest hope that I may be able to effect a cure."

The Doctor rang the bell. "Samuel, request the lady in the carriage to step into the house. Show her into the drawing-room. With your permission, Sir Nicholas, I will speak to her myself concerning your treatment?"

The Doctor was expecting to see an elegant, lady-like woman, something slender, and answering to the attenuated gentility of the being in whom "hope deferred, evindently made the heart sick."

What was his astonishment when he beheld a blooming, buxom, short, fat, merry-looking lass! with a face that sorrow seemed never to have smitten. She wore a large hat and feathers; such a profusion of rich brown hair,

sweeping down her back, as would have made the Lord
Chancellor the finest wig in the land.

It is needless to relate the conversation. The Doctor
soon found that she was desirous of becoming Lady
Nicholas Skinner, and very soon settled the matter with
great adroitness.

"*He must ride on horseback!* You must make him do so.
There is nothing the matter with him, but over anxiety to
be better; and it is all in your hands. You, and you only,
have the power of making him better."

"But about the wind?—state of the weather? what is
your advice? east, west, north, or south,—which is best?"

"No matter; the more wind the better gallop! Show
him the way over Salisbury Plains; and make him follow
you. Take no notice whatever of his feelings; but tell
him, if he feels for you, he must keep pace with you.
He will soon be better!"

"But, about horses? There are no good riding horses
in Salisbury."

"We will arrange that for you. Sir Nicholas may
leave that to me. Only assure him that he must per-
severe;—and let me know how he is, this day month."

At the end of the month, the Doctor received the
following epistles in one cover; evidently meant to be a
mutual acknowledgment.

Salisbury, August 1st, 1774.
"DEAR DOCTOR GAMBADO,—Love and wind have triumphed. The horses suited admirably ; though I fear the one Sir Nicholas rides is rather short-winded, as he comes to a stand still before we have had half a gallop. Still, I thank you, he is greatly improved. It was hard work, and seemed very cruel at first, but he himself will tell you the news.

"I remain, Dear Doctor Gambado,
Your's, gratefully,
CLARISSA DOUBLEDAY."

Salisbury, August 1st, 1774.
"DEAR DOCTOR,—I enclose a cheque for £300 upon my banker in town ; £200 for the horses, which are delightful creatures, and I thank you for obtaining them for us ; and £100 for the last fee to Doctors!—by far the best ; for I hope to be married in September. It is an ill wind that blows nobody good.

"But in love, and wind, I remain, Dear Doctor,
Your's obliged,—NICHOLAS SKINNER."
"Doctor Gambado,
Bread street, Cheapside, London."

> Love blows a blast, to conquer every man,
> Let him resist it,—long he never can ;
> 'T will conquer all, and in the end bring peace,
> Hurrah for love! true love can never cease!

CHAPTER V.

How to ride a Horse on three Legs.

FAME never permits her votaries to rest, and once a
man has gained a certain reputation for any thing,
he is wise who can be the humblest under it, because
he is conscious only of demerit.   Should Fame desert him,
he will never sink under it.   He will say, " I had a great
deal more than I deserved ; let me be content."   Wise
man indeed !   Doctor Gambado, however, found that
Fame did not desert him nor his practice.   He was the
more sought after, the more personally-retired he would
become.   Bread-street is not now celebrated for the
worthies it was an hundred years ago ; but there are
worthy men in it, and perhaps worthier than those an
hundred years ago, though not so celebrated for *ec-
centricities*.   Man's nature alters very materially under the
impression of time.   Men inveigh against fashion ; but
the most convenient fashion is that which is the simplest

LONDON   YORK & CARLISLE

Henry Bunbury Esq.r in.t

after all. Clerical habits alter; externally they go for a class, a profession, or degree. We hope that external feature will never be mistaken for internal; or the clergy would be black indeed. Quakerism used to be a badge of simplicity in dress and manners, till the self-possession of prosperity destroyed the equanimity of judgment; and men set them down for exactly their worth. But gently, my steed, gently; too long soliloquies generally make a man yawn.

Doctor Gambado had to go from London to York, and to visit no less a person than one of the greatest ecclesiastical dignitaries of the land, as the following letter will show.

"Precincts, York, October 10th, 1774.

"Sir,—Doctor Greathead is desirous of consulting you, as speedily as possible; and if you have an eminent veterinary surgeon, who can accompany you, the Doctor will pay all expenses, as he has a favourite horse very ill. Travel post, if you please.

I am sir, your humble servant,

George Gotobed, Hon. Sec. &c. &c."

Characteristic of simplicity was the Doctor's letter, that very instant, to John Tattsall, written on a scrap and sent by his own servant.

" John,—Will you be ready to start for York in an hour ?

" Your's,— Gambado."

John's reply was more laconic.

" Yes.

" Your's,—J. T."

In one hour see this loving couple off for York. Each confiding in the other's integrity, they each took plenty of money with them. At that time, travelling by post or by coach was no joke. In a general way, from London to York was a four days' journey ; but now, four hours will do great things.

We are not going to bother our readers with a description of all the adventures of these worthies on their way. How many times they were upset. How many times the post boy's horse fell down. How many spokes, fellies, or hobs, were splintered. Let it suffice that, with two such resolute men inside, who were never at a loss for contrivances under the very worst circumstances, they were sure to get safely through the journey.

Had the reader seen the blunderbuss,—yes, the bell-mouthed brass blunderbuss,—with a strange springing bayonet at the muzzle, the moment it was discharged, and this placed in the fore front of the carriage, directly opposite the sword case behind, he would indeed have said the Doctor was well provided against any robbers of the Yorkshire Ridings.

John, too, had a brace of pistols under his belt. They had no occasion, however to use them. They were conspicuous enough to every post-boy, waiter, and stable-keeper. Whether that kept them from an attack, we know not; but they were not attacked. and arrived safely at the then celebrated Precincts, close to the Cathedral.

They found the great Doctor Greathead, seated in an invalid chair, about four o'clock in the afternoon. His first words of salutation were those of hospitality.

"Gentlemen, have you had any refreshment after your journey?"

Doctor Gambado declared they had only just stept out of the carriage.

"Before I converse with the gentlemen, show them into the refectory. I will be prepared, half an hour hence, for our consultation."

Glad was Doctor Gambado, to refresh his stomach after travel, and not less glad John Tattsall to partake of the great divine's hospitality.

They did ample justice to the good things set before them; and as neither of them had any favour to ask of

this great man, but both had something to confer, they
were in no fear of taking too much or too little.

The butler was very attentive, and asked if they had
had any adventures upon the road.   Of course he received a courteous reply.   The Doctor inquired if there
was any thing new in York.   New York was then unknown ; but *York New Theatre* was then the go all over
the north.   It was just finished in most exquisite style,
and was in fact the lion of the north.

" You will have plenty to see, sir," said the butler, " if
you never were at York before.   Our Minster is the
wonder of the world."

" But your master, he must be a wonder ? "

Very few masters are wonders in their butler's eyes,
though many a butler becomes a wonder in the service of
his master.

" There is nothing very wonderful about my master,
except his present indisposition ; and I most sincerely
hope that your visit may do him good."

The butler had great respect for Doctors, and for
Doctors that had before them the title of Right Reverend,
or His Grace, or My Lord, or The Venerable; and these or
some of these, he was accustomed to see every day; but an
M.D. F.R.S. was not often in his view.   He had noted
these letters upon Doctor Gambado's card.   The other

gentleman had no card, and, therefore, he concluded that he was the greater man.

The footman came in to announce that his master was ready to receive Doctor Gambado and his friend.

There was something formidable in entering the presence of so great a divine as Doctor Greathead; but they were not going in for an examination of themselves, but to examine.

"Now, my friends, I can talk to you. I did not like talking to starving men, lest they should be ready to eat me up; and you will say, they would have enough to do to do that. But there are no cannibals at York, or I might have been eaten up long ago. Still, I regret to say that I have a disease preying upon my vitals; and except you can prescribe a cure, Doctor, I am afraid it is all up with me."

" We can prescribe no cure, without understanding the nature of the complaint."

" But it is that which puzzles the faculty in York. They say I have no bodily complaint; that it is all upon the *nerves*; and therefore it is, that in applying to my friend, Doctor Turnbull, to know if he knew any physician in London celebrated for his knowledge of the treatment of nervous cases, he mentioned you as the author of a book upon the nervous system; and I desired my secretary to write to you. You have well done to come to us, and we hope to receive benefit from your advice."

"I am obliged to Doctor Turnbull, for the mention of my name; but I must make some inquiries about your bodily health?"

"How is your appetite?" "Good."

"How is your sleep?" "Good."

"How is your sight?" "Good."

"How is your pulse?" "Try it."

"What do you say yourself?" "It is good."

"Have you any fever?" "None."

"Have you any particular pain?" "No."

"Do you walk much?" "No."

"Do you ride much?"

"I can ride no longer; and I fear this is one of the painful causes of my strange distemper."

"Are you accustomed to horse-back exercise?"

"Constant: I used to ride on the Carlisle road every day, till about a month since, and now I never ride."

"Why not?"

"I have lost the fancy or taste for it, and somehow I care no longer about it."

"Ah! that's bad! That's bad of itself. You met with no accident, to give your nervous system a shock, did you?"

"None whatever, except that my favourite old horse could go no longer, and I no longer felt inclined to go."

" But there are other horses that might be had equally as good "

"None, sir, None! I do not believe there is another horse in England that could carry me, like my old gray."

"If Yorkshire cannot suit you, I know no other county in the kingdom likely to do so. Surely, Doctor Greathead, you must be deceived in this respect?"

" Deceived or not, Doctor Gambado, I am not deceived in saying this, that I will ride no other horse; and, in fact, I would rather ride that horse on three legs, if he could be made to go upon them, then any other horse upon four."

Great men as well as little men have singular crotchets in their heads sometimes; and if these crotchets cannot be altered, they will go on in such a monotonous tone that they never get out of it. The Doctor was a learned scholar, and a very good divine; but his favourite horse was as dear to him as a lady's favourite cat or cap could be to her.

He had rode the same horse ten years, and had got so attached to him, that when that horse was seized with a lameness in the off hind leg, and could no longer stand or go upon it, the Doctor's sympathies increased with his favourite, though he was no longer any use to him.

Like his master, the animal fed well, and could sleep well,
but he could not go.

" Have you seen my horse ? "

" I came to see yourself first, Doctor, and I can have no
objection to go and see your horse, in company with my
friend Mr. John Tattsall, who I should say knows more of
a horse than any man living ; and can make a horse go,
I verily believe, on three legs."

The very idea gave animation to Doctor Greathead's
features.

" I will walk with you to the stables."

He rang the bell, ordered his hat, gloves, and even his
riding whip, so precocious was the idea that the Doctor
had conceived of being able to mount once more his
favourite gray.

The horse was led out, and came out upon three legs ;
the other evidently of no use to him.   In fact he could
not put it to the ground.

John examined the sturdy old fellow, who had a small
head and stout legs ; he pronounced him to be afflicted
with an incurable disease in the coffin-bone, and said he
never could go upon that leg.   He looked at all the other
limbs, and pronounced them *all right*.

" A fine old horse, your Reverence; a fine old horse, fit
to carry your worship's weight ; but he never will go
again upon all fours."

" Can he ever be made to go upon three ? "

" I see no reason to doubt it. The disabled limb is only such from the fetlock to the hoof; if the joint could be supported from the hock to the fetlock, and pressure be produced so as to keep that leg up to his body, without any weight falling upon the tendons of the foot, I see no reason why the horse should not canter upon three legs,—I do not say with the same ease as he would upon four sound ones ; but certainly easier far than he could upon the four as they now are."

" You are a sensible man, sir, and what you say seems feasible. What would you suggest ? "

" Let one of your grooms go and get a Yorkshire weaver's strap that will go once round the animal's body, and at the same time catch up the animal's leg,—and fasten it with a stout Birmingham buckle, so that the power shall be exerted in the leg bone without the fetlock or the foot; and I think your Reverence will be able to show to all the world *how to ride a horse on three legs.*"

" Good ! good ! Let it be done immediately : I verily believe it can be done."

It literally was done, and in one hour Doctor Greathead showed that he himself was alive again. He mounted his favourite gray ; and though the animal laid its ears, and lifted up its hind quarters, rather higher than usual, it

E

went; and did perform what the Doctor never expected
it to do again—namely, carried him a mile on the Carlisle
road, and that without a fall.

It did the Doctor good whenever he did ride it.
How often that was, we have no record to tell us.

He paid the Doctor of Medicine and his friend John
Tattsall more than would have purchased three fine Yorkshire horses.   In fact he paid for his whim.

He was cured of his whim.

And Doctor Gambado and his friend John returned
to town satisfied.

> If men have fancies, bugbears of the mind,
>   And money, too, to pay for what they want;
> Why should they not, like Doctor Greathead, find
>   Their fancies made to profit more than cant?
> We all have fancies! what more should we say,
> Than if we would indulge them, we must pay?

CHAPTER VI.

Tricks upon Travellers.

THE descent from the sublime to the ridiculous is a very easy transition in this mortal life. Even in the moments of utmost seriousness, we have seen something flit across the vision of the brain, or eye, or the spirit, that for a moment diverts the current of thought from the simplicity of the most devout and earnest Christian. Every moment we learn a new lesson of life and thought, from nature or from grace.

Thoughts are continually arising as to the probability of doing anyone any good, in these narratives. They form a diversion of thought, and much must depend upon the disposition of the mind of the reader. A good man will make some good out of every thing, and a bad man will find nothing good in anything.

To look simply at the picture, and to laugh at it, is easy; but to say, that they who played tricks upon others deserved to be whipped out of them, might be easier said than done.

Among the Doctor's patients was a singular mean old gentleman, Sir Abraham Crusty, who was recommended by the Doctor to ride out hunting, or to give the hounds a look, by way of diversion to his usual nothingness in his country-box. Sir Abraham had retired from city friends, city business, city thoughts,—to enjoy, as he hoped, the breezes and the green fields, and rural occupation at his country seat in Surrey; but being very hypochondriacal, and very mean as well, he was desirous of being as economical as possible, and not desirous of being considered a regular fox-hunter.

He could look on, enjoy the variety, and not be expected to pay anything towards the support of the hounds. Hence he would drop in upon them, look at them, ride a little way with them, and then return quietly to his own mansion. He would not keep a hunting stud, nor any man-servant to ride out with him. He was old enough to take care of himself, wise to do his own will, and mean enough to think about nobody else but himself.

When he consulted the Doctor, and was told what to do, he asked him if he could tell him the best way to do it. " Go to John Tattsall's, buy a steady hunter with good strong limbs, and one that will make no mistake."

He did so : but John mistook him for an old farmer,
and, consequently, gave him a good old hunter for a very
little money. Any body might take Sir Abraham Crusty
for what they pleased, so long as they did not take too
much of his money; and that he took care not to throw
away upon even saddle, bridle, or riding whip, for he rode
on an old saddle covered with a thick cloth, and had a
drover's cart whip for his hunting whip ; and few would
imagine Sir Abraham was going out to follow the hounds.
He used to go himself overnight to the King Charles in
the Oak, sleep there, and, as if he were merely a travelling
man of business, who came for lodging for man and beast,
he paid packman's fare for supper at night, and break-
fasted upon eggs and bacon in the morning ; and started
off quietly for the covert's side, without any intention of
being considered a hunter.

He went, however, one day with a very bitter complaint to Doctor Gambado, saying, he thought his horse
would be the death of him, for that he never started
from the Royal Oak without such a violent fit of kicking,
that he was afraid of a fall; and that made him so
nervous, he thought the Doctor ought to return him his
fee, and Mr. Tattsall take the horse back and allow him
something handsome for his keep of it.

"And so I will," replied the Doctor, "if John Tattsall do not cure him, or at least account for his kicking."

"Where do you say he exhibits these tricks," said John?

"At the Royal Oak, Norwood."

John was there the next Easter hunt day. So was Sir Abraham.

John saw him start, and saw that two urchins, viz. the post boy and the boots, stuck a stick under his tail, which seldom fell off until the old gentleman had had quite enough of the kicking. But once the stick dropped, the old horse went quiet enough.

When Sir Abraham was gone, John came from his dormitory, and soon put this question to the lads:

"Why do you treat that old gentleman in this shabby way?"

"Vy, sar, because he is a shabby, crusty old fellow, and treats all the sarvents of the hestablishment in the shabbiest vay. He pays for his bed, and for his 'orse's bed,—for his board, and his 'orse's board,—but he never gives Sal anything, vat beds him up at night, nor Bill anything, vat beds his 'orse up,—nor me anything, vat cleans his old boots for him; so ve just shows him vun of our tricks upon travellers: that's all, and sarves him right."

This was told to the Doctor, who, the next time he saw Sir Abraham, said to him :

"Sir Abraham, you will forgive my honesty ; but, if you wish to cure your horse of kicking at the Royal Oak, you must know how to be penny wise, and pay the chambermaid, the hostler, and the boots. I am sure you will never be pound foolish."

Sir Abraham took the hint, and the horse never kicked again at the King Charles in the Oak.

> To all their dues, let no man flinch to pay,
> If he would prosper in an honest way;
> Customs are good, if carried not too far,
> And a good custom, oft prevents a jar;
> Sir Abraham's horse no more gave out his kicks,
> Nor John nor Bill on travellers played tricks.

CHAPTER VII.

How to prevent a Horse slipping his Girth.

"MY dear Gambado," said Lord Rosier to the Doctor, "I know not how I shall ever repay you for your good advice. I am your debtor, for two things; first for inducing me to take up horseback exercise again, and then for recommending me to your friend John Tattsall, who has furnished me with a most excellent trotter, and one that does one good to ride it."

"I am glad to hear it, my Lord; but to what purpose is your visit to me this morning? You look the picture of health; I hope nothing is the matter."

"Oh! dear no! Nothing is the matter with me; but, I thought I might, without any intentional offence, just call and speak to you about the horse. I hope I do not offend."

"By no means, my Lord; pray go on. Your Lordship will not impute to me any thing wrong in the character of the horse?"

Henry Bunbury Esq.

" By no means, Doctor; by no means. I only sought your advice, because I thought you so skilful that you could get me into the right method of treating a horse."

" Humph ! "

This was the first direct slap at the Doctor's *veterinary powers*. He had a request from York to bring with him a *veterinary surgeon;* but he was now consulted by a British nobleman about the treatment of a horse. Well, thought the Doctor, let us hear the complaint; for after all it may be the fault of the rider more than of the beast.

" What is the matter, my Lord ? "

" It is simply this,—the creature, though in every other respect a suitable one, has a strange propensity or habit of slipping his girths ; so that when I have rode out a mile or two, I find myself upon his rump ; and once, indeed, I happened to let go the reins, and the saddle came over his tail, and I slipped off behind. He then quietly walked out of his saddle and went away, leaving me to carry my own saddle to the nearest hostelry, and to have a walk home, instead of a ride."

" My Lord, you acknowledge that it was your own fault for letting go the reins. Never, under any circumstances, let the reins go out of your own hands ; if you do, your are sure to have a fall. The same, my Lord, with all who hold the reins of government ; a tight rein can always be sufficiently slackened, when an improvement is required in the pace; but once let them entirely go, and you have no longer any power to guide. Your horse must run away, and you must have a fall."

"But what is a man to do, when he finds that the animal he rides gets the bit into his mouth, and bores so strongly upon his arms that it gives him the cramp in his muscles to hold the reins in his hands?"

"There you puzzle me. I confess, I should very soon give up riding such a horse altogether. But," said the Doctor, looking at his watch, "if you do not mind walking with me as far as Tattsall's, I think John could give you better advice upon this head than I can. Come, it is worth the trouble."

"With all my heart: I esteem it a favour. My groom shall lead the horse to his stables, and we will walk on after him."

The Doctor and his noble patient were soon in John Tattsall's yard.

"John, I have brought Lord Rosier to you, to learn a lesson. He is in a fix about a horse he bought of you, which he approves in every other respect but that of slipping his girth; can you tell the gentleman how to prevent it?"

"To be sure I can, Doctor, if the gentleman will only

condescend to give me a little attention. I will mount
the horse myself, and show him how I prevent the horse
from slipping his girths.' He did so ; and when he gave
up the horse, he said, "There, sir, observe what I have
done.

"Stick your feet, my Lord, home in the stirrups, press
all your weight thereupon, and so push the saddle
forward. If the horse bores upon your arms, bore him
well with your legs the moment he lifts his head; the
saddle, if it has slipped, will immediately regain its position.
And when he bores his head down again, you have nothing
to do but to repeat the boring him in his sides ; and as
the horse suits your Lordship so well, this will only form
a little agreeable variety of exercise for the benefit of your
Lordship's health; which I am heartily glad to find so
greatly improved."

"Thank you, John ; thank you, it will do, it will do!"

'Tis a bore, a horse to ride,
Slipping girths from side to side;
'Tis a bore with many pains,
For a man to lose the reins.

Keep your seat, and keep command,
And hold your bridle well in hand :
Fast and firm the steed will go,
And slips and slides you 'll never know.

CHAPTER VIII.

How to ride without a Bridle.

"DOCTOR, what am I to do?" said Mr. Broadcloth, the wealthy tailor of Bond-street. "Here am I, just fifty years of age, now in the prime of life, and cannot enjoy a moment's content. I have forty-nine hands at work for me, in my shop every day, beside piece-work out-doors. I have six runners of errands; four porters, to carry out my goods, and to bring me home work. Beside all this, I have such incessant customers to be measured, and coats to make, that from morning to night I hear nothing but snip go, snip go, snip go! and although I work like a journeyman, I half wish I was one of my own porters, and could go from house to house for fresh air and exercise."

"Oh, my dear sir!" said the Doctor, "you must ride on horseback,—you must indeed! you must be a journey-

Henry Bunbury Esq.r
27.

man yourself,—carry out your clothes to Clapham, and find yourself all the better in health and spirits."

"Doctor, I have heard that all who can do as you bid them, are sure to recover."

> "The first of all blessings is health,—for without it
> Men may think their's enjoyment in life,—but I doubt it."

"Then recover yourself, and you will own my advice to be good."

"What shall I do for a horse?"

"Do as everybody else does,— go to John Tattsall's, and get the horse that will suit you. I shall be glad to see you on one."

The tailor was soon mounted;—but it is one thing to be mounted,—another to be seated.

He soon complained to Mr. Tattsall, that the horse he had bought of him would not mind the bridle.

"Then," says John, "ride him without one. In fact, your horse did belong to a lame letter-carrier, and he never rode him with a bridle. You may have one round his neck by way of a check rein; but this horse, you will find, will never deceive you.

"You have nothing to do but to mount, and say, 'Go on:' he will be off in a gentle canter along the gutter, keeping close to the pavement, avoiding the lamp posts, oyster

stalls, orange tables, trucks, and barrows ; and whenever
you say 'Wo-ho,' he will make a dead stop. You may
get off, and wait an hour, if you like, he will never stir,
but will know how to take care of himself; only give him
a bit of carrot or an apple, just to let him know you are
his master, as the poor old lame duck did,—and you may
mount and say 'Go on,' and 'Wo-ho,' twenty times in a
day,—and he will obey you.   You will not need a bridle
or a rein."

Mr. Broadcloth did so,—and never complained of his
horse after,—and quite recovered of his complaint.

Go on !—wo-ho ! Good words will all command,
And gentle treatment bring the steed to hand.

Henry Bunbury Esq. inv.

R.C.

CHAPTER IX.

How to make a Mare go.

"ONEY makes the mare to go," is a very old proverb. Very few men have read the original peom upon this subject, except they have met with a very old volume of Crashaw's Poems.

> "Will thou lend me thy mare to go a mile?
> No, she is lame, leaping over a stile.
> But if thou wilt her to me spare,
> I'll give thee money for thy mare.
> Ho! ho! say ye so?
> Money makes the mare to go."

But one of the Doctor's patients was on old active fishmonger, of the name of Sturgeon; one well to do indeed in his line, a hundred years ago. There are a great many who now supply the London market, without any of that hard road work from Greenwich to Billingsgate. Now

trains run to and fro, and fish are alive in London from
the smacks.   But it was smack and go, then, with carts
every morning, one after the other in succession, loaded
almost top heavy.   Then there was unpacking, packing
and off for the coaches, Times, Phenomena, Telegraph,
Exeter Mail, Yorkshire Old Blue, and a host of others, to
supply provincial fishmongers, &c. and great houses in
the country.

But Mr. Sturgeon had, by command of his surgeon, to
drive no longer.   But Doctor Gambado insisted upon it,
that he must ride on horseback.   Now Mr. Sturgeon had
a very favourite mare, which could trot well in harness;
but could not be persuaded into any but a slow pace, if
any one rode on her back.

"What would I not give," he said to the Doctor, "if
she could be made to go."

"Well," said the Doctor, "money makes the mare to
go; and I have no doubt old John Tattsall, who was never
yet at a loss what to do with horseflesh, would soon put
you into the way of making your mare to go."

"What! with me on her back?"

"Oh, yes! and another besides, if wanted."

John was duly consulted.

"Well, Mr. Sturgeon, I see no difficulty in the matter.
It requires only a little courage on your part, and I am

sure you will find it answer you purpose well. You have
nothing to do, but exercise a little ingenuity in your own
line. When you are next at Greenwich, just take a good
strong lobster, with a pair of tremendous claws; fasten
him by the tail to the inside of your fishmonger's coat, and
let his head and clinchers hang out against the mare's
flank. Sit you firm in the saddle, with your feet well out
of the black pincher's way. One gripe, and the mare will
go like a shot; nor will she stop to let you pick up your
hat and wig; but wherever her stable is in town, you
will see she will never stop till she reaches it."
The trial was made, and

Away went Sturgeon, like a shot,—
Away, away! The mare could trot;
And so she did,—nor did she pause.—
John Tattsall gained the world's applause;
For one sharp bite upon the side,
And such a gripe of hair and hide,
The monster held within his claw,
That Sturgeon scarce could hold her jaw.
With head uplift, and leg up high,
The mare, like swallow, seemed to fly,
And soon, from Sturgeon's round bald pate,
The wig and hat flew o'er the gate;
But on rode Sturgeon, made to know
How well to make a mare to go.

F

CHAPTER X

The Tumbler, or its Affinities.

WE cannot narrate all the varieties of patients the Doctor had to deal with. We leave the ladies' cases out of the question, though he strongly recommended to them his great receipt—a ride on horseback.

Of all the difficult cases the Doctor had to deal with, was that of a little stingy, dyspeptic, middle aged pin-man, retired from business, and resident in Pimlico.

He was never satisfied. No one could convince him that he was not a good rider, though he had caused more broken-kneed horses in one month, than any other rider had made in twelve months. He literally went by the name of Tumble-down-Pincushion. It was no use furnishing him with a good horse; down it would come before long, and the little man would roll over like a

Henry Bunbery Esq.r inv.t

pincushion ; pick himself up, and declare it was the fault
of the horse.

He would exasperate his Doctor, and his Doctor's
friend, by pretending to show them how a man ought to
sit on horseback ; and truly, if ever there was a contrast
visible, it was in the upright figure of John Tattsall on
horseback, and Mr. Jeremiah Hinchman, the retired pin-
man of Pimlico. John always knew how to make the
most of a horse. Mr. Hinchman never did make any
thing but the least of himself and of his horse also.
There was a strange affinity between his horse and himself,—at least, between him and one, a favourite rat-tailed
sorrel gray. If it tumbled down, it was never disturbed :
it was so accustomed to the affinity with the ground, that
its knees became hardened with a species of horney excrescence, that seldom showed any thing but dirt, if it did
tumble. Nor did the little man either, for having a
remarkably light weight in the saddle, and a prominent
disposition to bend over his horse's neck, he generally
cast a very light summersault in his exit from the seat to
the ground.

"I wish," he said one day to Mr. Tattsall, in no very
amiable mood, "I wish you would put me in some way
of not falling off the tumble-down-horses which you
sent me."

"Sir," said Tattsall, "I would not let you ride a horse of mine, till you had paid for it as your own, or paid me the price of it, by way of insurance against the surety of his being a tumbler in your hands. You say you are suited with a very quiet tumbler, and one that takes it easy when he is down. You want yourself to be made to take it as easy as your horse; and, now, sir, to prove my readiness to serve you as a customer, and to serve you well too, I will put you into a way of having such affinity with your horse, that you shall tumble off no more."

"If you do," said Mr. Hinchman, "I will forgive you for having sent me twenty horses, not one of which could keep its legs, or keep me on his back."

John was not easily puzzled.

"Sir," said he, "you must manage the thing your own self. Only just hear my proposed plan. Let an incision be made in two places upon each flap of the saddle; let a thong pass under the saddle-flap, and tie it yourself over your knee. You will then never fall off; but be enabled to keep your seat until your horse shall rise again with ease, and you thus prove the truth of the motto

The Tumbler, or its Affinities.

Affinity is defined by Johnson, to be relation by

marriage, as opposed to consanguinity,—by others. as relation or agreeableness between things. No one . ₋uld think of Mr. Hinchman being of the same consanguinity as his horse Tumbler, but as a relation of agreeableness between two things, in this latter, the tumbler had his affinity with his master.

> Thus they kept the road together,
> Whether fine or foul the weather ;
> And when they tumbled, both went down ;
> And when they rose, they both weut on.
> So on they went, and all men's eyes
> Saw Tumblers with Affinities.

CHAPTER XI.

How to do Things by Halves.

THERE is an old saying, and generally considered a good one: "Never do things by halves." But there are exceptions to every rule, and the sending a bank-note by halves, is one of them ; and a very good exception too. We wish anyone who reads this, would only be induced to send to the Publisher half a bank of England note, and get it acknowledged by the Author, for the good work he has in hand, even in this publication ; and he will be sure to be rejoiced to receive the other half as well, and acknowledge that things done by halves, may answer a better purpose than the being done all at once.

Meet an old friend half way, and I'll warrant you they will go together the other half ten thousand times more pleasantly than if they had both met only at the journey's end. Still, in a general way, things done by halves do not always fit, so as to make the whole agreeable. They

Henry Bunbury Esqr. inv.

may become so conjoint as to be agreeable to each other; but who does not like to see a good house built all at once, rather than patched from time to time? Who likes to see a church half restored, and half a ruin? So, who likes to have half the heart of his sweetheart, and never to have the whole. Let him learn to have a whole heart himself, first, and he will be sure to possess the whole heart of another, and fulfil the whole law.

Alderman Goodbeheard, who had been one of Doctor Gambado's patients, delighted, when in the country, to see the hounds; but being a very portly person, and not one of the highflyers in the field, he told John Tattsall, that he wanted a horse that would get over gates and styles, without taking a flying leap. He must have one that could creep over them, by putting first his forelegs on, and then his hind, so as to give him time to lean forward and to lean backward, without those sudden jerks, which he had seen some gentlemen get in the saddle. He did not mind his horse breaking a bar or so, provided he did no mischief to himself or to his rider; for, as the Alderman generally rode along convenient roads and footpaths, he wished to do so with comfort to himself and convenience to his creature.

"I see, sir," said John; "you want a creeper, that will do things by halves."

"Exactly so, sir! exactly so, sir!"

"I can suit your worship well, only you must keep a whip, constantly to ride behind you, just to teach the animal to do as he was taught, to do things by halves."

"If you can find me a lad to do this, I should be glad to have him in my service."

"I have a groom in my service, who would just suit your purpose. He has, in fact, been the trainer of the animal to do just that kind of thing."

"Capital! capital! I will furnish him with scarlet coat and cap, boots and spurs, whip and saddle, and pay him £2 2s. per week, until the end of the hunting season, when you may have him again to train other horses how to do things by halves."

So paid the Alderman his groom,
And found in hunting he had lost his gloom;
For though, by halves, the hunter's work was done,
The master and his man both shared the fun.

Henry Bunbury

CHAPTER XII

Doctor Cassock, F.R.S. I.P.Q.

DOCTOR Cassock was, in his day, a most extraordinary man : he was a double-first at Oxford, a scholar, and a gentleman. He was a most benevolent little man, and Doctor Gambado's friend and pastor, both well read and well bred. But he was ever cultivating his inventive faculty to do good. In his visits to the poor, he invented new bed-rests, new cradles, new spring beds, new comforts of every kind. He was a great inventor of puzzle locks,—puzzle keys,—puzzle cupboards, doors, window frames, and fire-guards. In short there was, as he used to say, no device in the grave ; therefore, he was ever starting something new.

Many a mechanic was indebted to him, and many a printer,—for in his church of St. Mildred's, in the Poultry, he was the first to put aside the old English black-letter character of the Bible and Prayer-book, and to assume

the type, which holds fast in all good printing-offices to
the present day. His sermons were always new, and were
the only things in which he might be said to puzzle nobody; for they were plain, simple sermons of solid truth
and practical utility.

He loved every soul, and being an acknowledged well-
read scholar, he was more popular among his people than
anyone who tried to gain popularity. His inventive
faculty, had it been in the present age, instead of one
hundred years ago, might have procured him the celebrity
of a Brunel, and a fortune; but his scheming being
always for others, he at last puzzled or puddled his own
affairs so as to involve himself and his means in dif-
ficulties; and becoming very low spirited, the friend of
others had to go and consult Doctor Gambado, and to
tell him at once that he came to be a charity patient,
for he had not a guinea in the world to give him.

"My dear, Cassock," said the Doctor, "in carrying
out your various projects, you have forgotten that learning
and wisdom should be joint companions; that they are of
little worth when separate, but of inestimable value when
united."

"You speak truth, my dear Gambado; and I find, by
experience, that a word of wisdom will often go further
than a purse full of guineas. Quite right. But you have

known me long enough to observe, that I have ever
thought the practical part of my profession superior to
all the learned part."

"That may be true. But, Doctor, you have not confined either your teaching or your practice to the duties
of your profession. I deny not that you have done good
to many. You have done me a great deal of good ; for,
to a certainty, I never knew you preach one thing and
practice another. Yet, sometimes, I have known you
interest yourself so deeply in imaginary inventions, as to
persuade yourself that you were doing good, when you
were entirely mistaken."

The Doctor sighed, and simply said, "Gambado, we
can never all think alike, any more than we can all be
alike. You have done right and made your fortune; while
my coat is threadbare, and I begin to want."

"All, believe me, Doctor, is as it should be. You
want my advice gratis. I always have had yours gratis,
and profitted by it, and loved it. Now, if you will take
my advice, I will take yours, and so we shall find mutual
accommodation."

"What is your advice ?"

"Ride on horseback."

"How can I do so ? One hundred pounds in debt, and
only one hundred pounds per annum. I cannot starve

a year, and ride on horseback too. You give advice I cannot follow."

"I should be sorry to do so. I will write you a prescription, but you must take it yourself to be made up in Lombard-street; and I will write you a note, which you must take to Mr. John Tattsall.

"Just read that paper, while I write the prescription, Doctor Cassock.

"Messrs Gold, Silver, and Company, Bankers, Lombard-street. Pay the bearer £100 on account of,

"Your's, faithfully,

£100.   GEOFFERY GAMBADO."

"DEAR JOHN,—Give my old friend, Doctor Cassock, just such a nag as the first I had of you for £50, and I will pay you for it,—for its keep, and for its stable room,—groom and all,—so that the Doctor may always find it saddled and bridled, and have nothing to pay; but set all down to the account of,

"Your's at command,

GEOFFERY GAMBADO."

"Mr. John Tattsall."

A tear rose to the eye of Doctor Cassock, as his friend handed to him both the notes ; and he felt that species of choaking sensation, which a good man feels at the un-expected generosity of a real friend.

" Oh, Gambado ! what advice can I ever have given to you, worthy such generosity as this ? "

" My dear old friend, I will tell you at once that I only follow out the text upon which you preached yesterday :

" ' Whatsoever ye would that men should do unto you, even so do unto them : for this is the law, and the prophets.' I have only done as I would be done by."

The Doctor could only say, " God bless you."

He was soon after enabled to repay the Doctor ; for a distant relation left him an independence, a few weeks after ; and he became the merriest, if not the wisest, old gentleman of his day.

He could not, even then, leave off the faculty of in-vention ; for he became the noted inventor of a noble puzzle, for Tumble-down horses. He was actually in-duced to take out a patent for it. He never found any body but himself to use it. He did use it, though in his case it never was wanted, for his horse never tumbled down with him ; and he put everyone who saw him

riding with it, in such a merry mood, that it was difficult
to say which laughed the heartiest, the Doctor himself, or
those who beheld him.

> A friend in need is a friend indeed ;
>   If you find him, own his worth ;
> He has never a word, but 'tis always God speed,
>   From the east to west, from south to north ;
> Do good to all, and do evil to none,
> And do to others,—what should be done.

Henry Bunbury Esq.

CHAPTER XIII.

A Daisey Cutter, with his Varieties.

IN the month of July, 1780, Doctor Geoffery Gambado was visited, from Birmingham, by the celebrated cutler, Mr. John Green, a gentleman who had
become uncommonly dyspeptic from a great excrescence,
wart, or wen, that grew out of his right temple, almost
covering his ear. It gave him no particular pain, except
when he chanced to recline upon that part of his head;
yet, as every body looked at it, who came into his shop,
and when he appeared at church, or in any public place,
he grew uncommonly irritable and nervous. The faculty
pronounced it too large to be cut out; and, if the truth be
told, Mr. Green himself had such a horror of cutting,
that, though a dealer in cutlery and in the very first steel
articles, he had an unconquerable distaste to the knife
being used upon his own person.

Like many other good kind of men, he dealt in articles

that others might use ; but he himself had no wish to
use them. Those who use the sinews of men, that is, of
other men, for their own speculative purposes, and actually abhor the use of the very things they sell, should
be careful of the exciting, inciting, or foolish words they
utter, lest their language should superinduce others to
use those articles in which their traffic is, to their own
destruction.   Mr. Burton, the great Quaker, was a dealer
in Burton ale to a great extent, though he was himself a
rigidly abstemious man ; yet, as his trade was a good one,
and paid well both in the north and south, he could
afford to give considerable sums to temperance, or even
total abstinence societies, without feeling any loss in his
trade.   The fact is, until the bright men of traffic shall
find out that the ruling principle of their souls is
coveteousness, they will never reform the world by a
spurious profusion of words and calculations, which have
only that one principle to appeal to as their own support.

Mr. Green dealt in swords, and knives and forks, in
guns and pistols, in lancets and razors ; but he would not
suffer the lancet or the knife to touch his own flesh.   He
was a dealer in weapons, not in blows.   A man of peace,
yet, like many a man styling himself a friend to humanity,
and assuming apostolic liberty, he could find fault with
every thing and every body ; yet, for trade's sake, he had

no objection to the demand for swords, guns, or pistols. He could supply the government with any quantity from his stores in Birmingham.

It must be confessed, that his nervous affection, and melancholy disposition arose more from the wart upon his brow, and all its external irritations, than from any qualms of conscience, arising from any kind of self examination, self accusation, or self condemnation. Few men's consciences so trouble them in the day of their prosperity.

He was recommended to consult the great nervous Doctor of the age, Doctor Gambado. So he went to town, had an interview with the Doctor, described all his agitating ails, and received this advice:

" Ride on horseback."

" But do you think that will do me any good ? "

" I am quite sure it will do you some good,—to what extent it is impossible to say,—that must depend upon your patience and perseverance. One thing you can always do, namely, wear a hat that will cover the appearance of the excrescence, and I should not be surprised at its being the means of reducing its size considerably."

Little did the Doctor himself imagine how a cure, by his advice, was completely effected.

" Oh, Doctor ! " exclaimed Mr. Green, " what would I not give could it be entirely eradicated by such gentle

G

means as horseback exercise. I am no great rider, but I would ride any distance, and almost any horse, to get rid of this awkward protuberance."

"Well, my dear sir, we will try. Nothing like trying."

"I have heard, Doctor, that you have large stables, and keep horses of all kinds."

The Doctor could not help smiling when he thought of his own fame, as a horse keeper, horse doctor, and horse furnisher.

"I have large stables at the back of my house, and I have three horses of my own ; but I never kept one for sale, or sold one myself. I let off my stables to a livery-keeper, who has ten or a dozen horses here , namely to Mr. John Tattsall, who has the credit of being able to suit everyone, only each must pay well to be suited."

"I should not mind what I had to pay, if I could be suited to my mind."

"Let us go and give him a look. If you can at all describe to him the sort of horse you want, I think he will soon be able to accommodate you. You may be sure, if the horse can be had, he will get it for you, if it is not at this time in his stable."

The Doctor's fee was cheerfully paid, £10 10s. neatly wrapt up in tissue paper. He had been told nothing less could be expected from a master cutler.

Mr. Green put on his large slouchy broad-brimmed hat that covered half his face ; and the Doctor and his patient were soon in the presence of the great Mr. Tattsall.

"John, this gentleman wants a horse."

"Glad of it, sir. Pray what sort of horse do you want, sir ? "

"A good one."

"Every body wants that, and I have a great many good 'uns ; ' but I like to know the sort of good 'un that a gentleman requires. One man likes a bay, another a gray, another a roan, another a chestnut ; but the colour is not always the description. One likes a high action, another a gentle goer, another a thunderer, another a prime bang up ; one likes a thorough-bred, another a hunter ; some require cobs, others carriage horses, others ladies' horses, others park horses ; but if you can describe the sort of animal you want, I can soon tell you if I can suit you."

"I did once see a horse," said Mr. Green, evidently calling up to his recollection days long gone by ; "I did once see a horse that made me say to myself, 'There ! if ever I ride on horseback, I should like to get just such a horse as that.' It was gentleness and elegance personified. It was a beautiful creature. It turned out its toes, just lifted one foot above the other, with a kind of quick

cross action, and then set it down with such elegance and
ease, that it seemed to trip along over the ground, exactly
like a dancing master.   Proud was its bearing, head up,
and tail high," and Mr. Green most poetically described it
in these words :

> "It brushed the morning dew,
> And o'er the carpet flew,
>   With all becoming grace.
> So gentle, and so nobly bred,
> Give it alone its upshot head,
>   'Twould go at any pace."

"Sir, I perceive you are a poet."

"Not a bit of it.   I only cut them out of the Poet's
Corner, in the Star, and I think the author's name was
' Anon ; ' but it mattered not as to who was the author, it
described the very horse ; and I thought then, and I think
so still, that by a very short transposition it would suit
my wife, and perhaps many others.   What think you,
sir ? "

> " She brushed the evening dew,
> And o'er the carpet flew,
>   With all becoming grace.
> So gentle, and so nobly bred,
> Give her alone her upshot head,
>   She'd go at any pace."

The Doctor and the dealer could not help laughing.

"I perceive, sir, you are a wag; if you are not a poet. I congratulate you upon having so charming a creature for your wife; and I only wish I may be able to suit you with as good a horse."

"Have you a horse of this description?"

"I have a mare exactly of that kind, and we call her the Daisy Cutter."

"Pray, let me see her."

"Shall I ride her, to show you her qualities?"

"If you please."

"Bring out the Daisy Cutter."

She was brought forth, and John soon set her off to advantage.

"Just the very thing! Just the very thing! Will you send her down to Birmingham? I am not exactly in riding trim, or I would ride her down myself."

The animal was paid for, sent home, and proved to be the very creature suited to Mr. Green's case.

He rode his celebrated Rosenante every evening, and greatly improved in bodily health. He actually became cheerful, and his wife blessed the good Doctor Gambado for having restored her husband to himself again.

Alas! for human infirmities, or for human vagaries! One of the most wonderful complaints of nervous hypo-

chondriacism, was actually cured, together with its cause,
by a momentary spree.

One beautiful evening, the little man was riding in the
gaiety of his heart toward Aston Hall, visions of future
greatness passing before his eyes, when, just upon the
greensward in front of the park gates, there lay in his
way a great black hog, on the very edge of the road. He
thought within himself, that he should like to take a leap
smack over the animal's back; and just looking round to
see that no eye should behold his spree, he gave his
" Rosenante " an unwonted kick with his heels.

She was certainly surprised at her master's unwonted
action, and in the spurt of the moment, cocked her tail,
lifted her head, and quickened her pace;—but whether
she did not see the hog, or could not leap over it if she
did, she ran directly over the animal, and fell over it,
awaking it in a horrible fright to scamper grunting
away;—but, alas! she pitched her own head, and her
master's head also, without his hat, upon the hard road.
They both went the whole hog.   Mr. Green lay senseless
on the road, in a pool of blood, arising from the severity
of the blow, which tore away the whole scalp of the
forehead, together with the entire wart or excrescence
which grew thereupon.   His Rosenante affrighted, returned to Birmingham,—was soon recognized,—and Mr.

Green was soon carried insensible to the hospital. He remained there some days, recovering himself and his senses.

Thus the Daisy Cutter and his vagaries became a proverb in Birmingham. And that which skill could not, or rather through nervous apprehension was not, permitted to try, a black hog, one of the most unlikely things in the world, was instrumental in effecting.

When spirits mount in cheerful glee,
Beware of leaping for a spree ;
    For sprees create a fall :
And when you leap alone in-cog,
Beware of going the whole hog ;
    Better not go at all.
Yet sometimes good from ill may spring,—
    One spree may prove satiety :
If Daisy Cutters wisdom bring,
    Rejoice in the variety.

CHAPTER XIV.

A Horse with a Nose.

DID any one ever see a horse without a nose? It cannot, therefore, be meant, at the heading of this chapter, to draw any distinction between a horse with a nose, and a horse without one. We say of a dog, he has got a good nose; that is, if, as hound, pointer, or retriever, he can scent or find his game *well*. A man we have seen without a nose, and a very painful sight it is to see any feature of the human face in any way distorted; but that such a man can " smell a rat," denotes not that he has a peculiar quality of scent, but that he is a cunning fellow, and can look a little deeper into the artifices of men and their motives than others are aware of. Some men have indeed the smoothest faces, and the simplest manners, and yet retain the utmost cunning, or, if men like it better, wisdom in the world. They can smell a rat,—they can discover a flaw in the indictment,—

AT LAST

Henry Bunbury Esq.ʳᵉ inv.ᵗ

they can see how an adversary may be overthrown, and
can quietly stir up strife and pick the pocket of friend or
foe, without of course doing any thing wrong; defrauding
any one, or in any way letting the sufferer himself suppose that he is the victim or tool, or goose to be plucked
by the cunning craft and subtlety of the deceiver.

If men will ruin themselves, whose fault is it? but, if
they do so, there are plenty to rise upon their ruin, and
to laugh at their folly. Conscience, they say, makes
cowards of all men; but that conscience must be founded,
not upon any man's judgement, but their own. There
never was any man who did no wrong that could be
afflicted by his own conscience; but there never was a
man, who by his own unaided judgment, ever did right so
perfectly, that his conscience could entirely acquit him of
every base and sordid motive. Many may be very highly
honourable and upright men, and yet have a great many
rogues to deal with, and scarcely know how to deal with
them. The best way is to say nothing, but avoid them.

Doctor Gambado had a patient come to him of this
kind, and he was a lawyer who stood *very, very* high in his
station one hundred years ago.

He was provokingly ill,—ill in his body,—ill in his
mind,—ill at ease with himself,—and dreadfully afflicted
with such disturbed thoughts at night, that his sleep went
from him, and his conscience had no rest.

It is very provoking to have a troublesome conscience ;
but it is more provoking still, not to be able to quiet that
conscience by any common or uncommon means. Simon
Deuce, Esq. who actually attained the eminence of high
authority, not in the court of Conscience, or in the court
of Equity, but in Chancery, had retired from business
and left his son-in-law, Sir Charles Dubious, his house in
Billiter-square. He himself took a mansion on Blackheath, and there he sought in vain for that enjoyment of
rest and contentment, which good men only inherit in
their latter end.

Physic was in vain,—advice, such as most men give,
produced no cessation of anxiety. He became moody,
sullen, morose, irritable, dogmatic, and all but absolutely
irrational. His faculties were piercingly sound, his
memory most acute, his legal knowledge clear, and his
discovery of transgressions of law were every day dis-
played before his eyes, from those who rode in a coronetted
barouche, to those who rode in a donkey cart. He loved,
actually loved to make complaints, and to see the law
carried out ; and in petty acts of tyranny he was so
absolute a persecutor, that he was a terror to all who
lived around him.

Generosity was never in his nature, neither did he ever
pretend to teach it, or observe its laws. In fact, every
one was considered by him as a weak fool, who did either

a kind or generous act, beyond the positive obligation of the law.

What happiness could such a man have in his retirement? His great happiness was the accumulation of money in the funds, and these occasioned him a momentary excitement. His friend, Samuel Ryecross, of Ryecross-house, Blackheath, advised him to consult Doctor Gambado.

" Do you mean Gambado, the horse dealer ? "

" He is not a horse dealer."

"I say he is a horse dealer, and ought to take out a licence for horse dealing. He does not do so, and I have half a mind to have him up, and bring him into court for cheating, defrauding, and robbing the government."

" I think you must have been misinformed. I believe he is really a very clever, honest man, and gives good sound practical advice to all his patients."

" Yes, so I have heard ; and all of it is ' Ride on horseback.' If I went to consult him, I should only get that advice. I know it before hand, and have no inclination to throw away a guinea for it."

" But is it bad advice in your case ? would it not do you good to try it ? Why, if you know his remedy, do you not pursue it ? "

" Because I do not think it would do me any good."

" Well, you have tried a great many doctors.   Let me
drive you in my phaeton to Bread-street, and let us hear
what the Doctor says."

" Will you pay the Doctor ? "

" Yes, if you will follow his advice."

" Done, we will go."

They did go.

The Doctor knew the man he had to deal with, and yet
he had confidence in the horseback exercise as the best
cure for him, and he told him so.

" Have you got a horse that would suit me ? "

" There is a fine strong horse in my stables, that I think
would suit you."

" May we go and look at him ? "

" I will go with you."

Samuel Ryecross was rather surprised ; but Simon
Deuce gave him a look, as much as to say, '*I told you he was
a horse dealer.*'

When they went to the stables, John Tattsall was there
himself, and not being known to either of the gentlemen,
they both supposed him to be the groom in the employ of
Doctor Gambado.

" John, I have brought a customer to look at the great
brown horse.   Is he at home ? "

" He is, sir ; I will lead him out."

He led him out,—rode him,—and Mr. Deuce asked the Doctor what his price was. The Doctor said, "John, what did you say the horse was worth?"

"Ninety guineas, sir, and not a farthing less. I would not let the gentleman have him for one guinea less."

"Will you order him to be sent to my house on Black-heath?"

"Shall I ride him there now, and bring back your cheque?" said John Tattsall.

"You may, if you please, my man."

John bowed, and after ascertaining the name of the abode, Billiter house, Blackheath, he rode off.

"In what name, Doctor, shall I write the cheque?" for, presuming that the Doctor was not professionally a horse dealer, though he considered that he had bought the horse of him, he had a mind to see if he shrunk at all from the responsibility.

The Doctor replied, "In the name of the very man who delivers him, John Tattsall; and I hope the horse will suit you, sir, and do you good."

"There," said Mr. Deuce to his friend Ryecross, "what say you now to the Doctor dealer? hey! Is not my deal with him this day sufficient to convict him before any bench of Magistrates in all the counties of England. If I do not take the shine out of this Doctor Gambado, then say that Simon Deuce knows nothing of the law."

When they got home, the horse had arrived.

The cheque was written :

"Pay John Tattsall," &c. &c.

John touched his hat, walked off with his money, took a cab to Lombard-street, got the cheque cashed; and called and thanked the Doctor for his recommendation.

The very next day, the Doctor received a summons to answer the charge of being a horse dealer without a licence for that purpose. The suit was preferred in the name of Deuce *v*. Gambado.

Of course, all these things are put into regular process of law, with which we shall not entertain the public. In due time, the case came on in the proper court, and Mr. Deuce swore that he bought such a horse of Doctor Gambado, and that the Doctor's servant, John Tattsall, delivered the horse at Billiter-house, Blackheath. Samuel Ryecross was witness to the transaction. The cheque was produced in court, and Mr. Deuce was lauded very highly for his sense of justice in not allowing the government to be defrauded, and more in not allowing that highly respectable profession of M.D. F.R.S. to be a covering to the tricks and degradation of a horse dealer without a licence.

Never, however, was Deuce more confounded in all his life, than by the cross examination of Serjeant Sharp.

" Pray, sir, may I ask—Did you go to consult Doctor
Gambado for any complaint ? "

" I went purposely, by the advice of my friend, Samuel
Ryecross."

" For what purpose, Mr. Deuce ? "

" To consult him."

" Were you ill at that time ? "

" Decidedly not well."

" May I ask the nature of the complaint for which
you consulted so eminent a physician as Doctor Gambado ? "

Mr. Deuce hesitated.

" I have no desire to know more of the complaint than
you may think right to tell us ; but all who have heard of
Doctor Gambado's patients, know well that they are
mostly afflicted with nervous depression. May I ask if
such was your case ? "

" Yes, it was."

" You were deranged, sir ; were you not ? "

Mr. Deuce, with great vehemence, " No more deranged,
sir, than you are."

" Do not be angry, sir, when I used the term *deranged*.
I meant that your system was a little deranged, disorganized, or so out of sorts, as to produce a kind of

physical disarrangement of the organs leading to the brain, so as to create unpleasant sensations, dyspeptic habits, sleepless nights, and a little of that irritability which we have just seen, so as to render you a little impulsive, and not unlikely to be mistaken."

Deuce did not like this at all, but he could not help saying

" It might be so."

" Oh! It might be so! Now, Mr. Deuce, I must put rather a strong question to you :

" Did you ever accuse Doctor Gambado of being a horse dealer ? "

" Not that I am aware of."

" Not that you are aware of! Now, sir, I must get you to tax your memory, and I ask you plainly, did you not go on purpose to trap Doctor Gambado into the selling you a horse, that you might bring him into a court of justice ? "

Mr. Deuce paused. He did not reply. He seemed nervous.

" Pray, sir, take your time. You are a member of the law, you know the law, and the usages of a court of justice ; and I am sure you will give us a plain, straight-forward answer."

" I did not go exactly with that intention. My friend,

Mr. Ryecross, persuaded me to consult him about myself."

"Now, sir, I shall cross-examine your friend, Mr.
Ryecross. Did you or did you not, at the very time that
you went to consult this eminent physician, say to your
friend, that he, meaning Doctor Gambado, was a horse
dealer, and not a physician?"

" I might have so said."

" Pray, sir, do you understand the law of libel? I
shall strongly recommend my client, let the result of this
action be what it may, to bring an action against you, sir,
for one of the grossest acts of libellous intention this
court has ever heard of; and, if I mistake not the judgement this day will decide, whether a gentleman like
yourself is to utter a libel of a ruinous tendency to so
high a professional man, with impunity.

" Then you did say he was a horse dealer?"

" Yes, I did."

" Pray, sir, had you any previous acquaintance with
Doctor Gambado?"

" None whatever."

"Then, I presume you acted in this manner entirely
upon hearsay evidence?"

" I certainly did."

" You had no quarrel with Doctor Gambado?"

H

" None whatever."

" Was it a sense of justice to your country, that entirely induced you to try and *smell a rat* in this gentleman's character ?

" It was."

" And on that account you laid this information against him ? "

" I did."

" It was not from any morbid indulgence of any splenetic humour with which you were at that time afflicted, that induced you to bring this action ? "

" Oh, dear, no ! "

" I may say then, sir, you considered it entirely pro bono publico ? "

" Quite so."

" You have told the court, sir, that you purchased the horse of Doctor Gambado ? "

" I did so certainly."

" You are sure he sold it to you ? "

" I am quite sure."

" Pray, sir, did you ask him, if the horse was his that you bought ?

" I asked him if he had any horse that would suit me."

" What was his reply ? "

"To the best of my knowledge, it was that he had one in his stables that would suit me."

"Now, sir, did he say, that *he had a horse* in his stables that would suit you?"

"I understood him so."

"Pray, Mr. Deuce, be sure; because I should be sorry to convict you of a wilful and direct falsehood. I pray you to be sure. Did he say *he had a horse that would suit you?* or did he say, *there was a horse in his stables that would suit you?*"

"It never struck me before,—he might certainly say, *there was a horse*; but I took him to mean, that *he had one* that he could sell me."

"Come, sir, I am very glad to find that you have a disposition to correct the evidence you have given for the prosecution. You have sufficient legal acumen to distinguish between a man saying, *there is such a horse,* and *I have such a horse;* the latter sentence would go to identify the ownership of the horse, or a declaration to that effect."

"He might then say, *there was a horse in his stable?*"

"Well, I think he did say so."

"And you did not ask whether the horse was his or not?"

"I did not."

Let Mr. Samuel Ryecross be called.

"You are the friend of the last witness,—are you not?"

" I am."

" You have known him for some years?"

"I have."

"Did you persuade him to consult Doctor Gambado?"

"I did."

"Upon what grounds?"

" Because of his dyspeptic habits."

" Did they not almost amount to monomania?"

" I considered that at times they did?"

" Was he not very splenetic?"

" Very."

" I ask you, if he has not, in the neighbourhood of Blackheath, the character of being very litigious?"

" He is very unpopular."

" He quarrels with everybody?"

" He makes himself conspicuous for finding fault with all transgressors of the law."

" Is he not very angry?"

" He is very easily provoked."

" Now, sir, I think, when you proposed to consult Doctor Gambado, that he objected?"

" He did so."

" Upon what grounds?"

" Upon grounds that would, if true, disqualify any medical man, for professional consistency."

" What were these grounds ? "

" He said he was a mere horse dealer,—that he would give him advice to ride on horseback, and would sell him a horse to do so."

" Did you believe his assertion ? "

" No. I not only doubted it ; but stoutly contradicted it."

" You had a better opinion of Doctor Gambado ? "

" I had."

" Now, sir, did not your friend actually say to you, that he would have the fellow up, meaning Doctor Gambado, for being a horse dealer without a licence ? "

" He did."

" Did he not go to the Doctor with that intent ? "

" I verily believe he did ; but I certainly did not accompany him with any such intent."

" You recommended him purely for his health ? "

" I did ; and, moreover, I paid the Doctor's fee, upon the promise that he would follow the Doctor's advice."

" Are Mr. Deuce's habits penurious ? "

" Extremely so."

" Then how comes he to be so litigious ? "

" He finds that costs him very little, if any thing in the end."

" He considers, then, in this case, that my client will be mulcted in costs ? "

" I have no doubt he does."

" Were you present when he consulted Doctor Gambado ? "

" I was."

" What was his advice ? "

" Ride on horseback."

" Did you consider that good advice ? "

" I did."

" What question did your friend put to the Doctor about the horse ? "

" He asked him, ' *Have you got a horse that will suit me ?* ' "

" What was his reply ? "

" There is a fine strong horse in my stables, that I think would suit you."

" Are you sure that was his reply ? "

" Quite sure."

" Did you consider that reply as affixing the ownership of the horse to himself ? "

" I confess that I did so."

" Did you see any triumphant glance, or recognition of Mr. Deuce's sagacity, at having fulfilled the declaration of the accuser, that he was a horse dealer ? "

" Yes, I did."

" Did you think the horse was the Doctor's own ? "

" I own, I did."

" Did you ask him if the horse was his? "

" No, I did not. I concluded it was so."

" Did you see the horse sold ? "

" I did."

" Who do you consider sold the horse ?

" I considered, to my great surprise, that Doctor Gam-bado sold the horse."

" Then you altered your opinion of the Doctor."

" I did so, considerably."

" Was your friend very warm upon the subject of the Doctor's horse dealing ? "

" Very."

" Did you know of his resolution to bring this action ? "

" I fully considered he would do so."

Mr. John Tattsall was then called.

" You are a horse dealer?

" I am."

" You know both the plantiff and defendant ? "

" I know the former, from having sold him a horse. I have known the latter many years."

" Pray, sir, do you hire Doctor Gambado's stables ? "

" I hire stables of Doctor Gambado."

" How far from your own stables? "

"The back premises of each join."

" How long have you hired the Doctor's stables ? "

" Fifteen years."

" How many horses do you generally keep there ? "

" Ten, twelve, fourteen, and sometimes sixteen horses."

" Pray, are you in partnership with Doctor Gambado?"

" No, I am not."

" Has he any share in your business ? "

" None whatsoever."

" Has he any horses ? "

" Three of his own."

" In a separate stable ? "

" In a stable adjoining to those I hire of him."

" To your knowledge, did the Doctor ever sell a horse ? "

" Never."

" Has he any horses to sell ? "

" None."

" You positively affirm upon oath that the Doctor is not a horse dealer ? "

" I swear it."

" Did he ever sell a horse for you ? "

" Never."

" Did you ever authorize him to sell a horse for you ? "

" Never."

" Pray was the horse that the plantiff, Mr. Deuce, bought, your property or the Doctor's ? "

" Mine."

" Did the Doctor give the price of the horse to the gentleman, or did you ? "

" I did,—the Doctor asked me what I had said was the price of the horse, and I told him,—and I told the gentleman I would not take one guinea less for him than ninety guineas."

" Then, really and truly, you took the money for your own horse, kept it, and did not give the Doctor a farthing ? "

" I gave him nothing but 'Thank you, Doctor, for introducing to me a customer.' "

" Had the Doctor seen the horse before ? "

" Frequently, and admired him for the strength of his limbs, and for his proportions."

" Do you remember what he said, when he brought the gentleman into your or his yard ? "

" Yes. 'John, I've brought a customer.' "

" You knew what that meant ? "

" Of course I did, and I led out the brown horse myself, and paced him, sold him, took the money; the cheque is, I suppose, in court : it was written for me, and

I had no idea the horse was sold by anybody but me, to whom it belonged."

At this stage of the proceedings the solicitor for the prosecution intimated that his client wished to withdraw his case.

Serjeant Sharpe said, " He hoped his Honour would direct a verdict for the defendant, his client; and that the world would see what a shameful action it had been. He told the solicitor for the prosecution that he was glad that his client felt ashamed of himself. He could never make him amends for what he had done; that it was disgraceful in the extreme to seek the advice of so good a man, and to treat him in the way he had done. He was quite sure that he would shortly have an increase of his malady, and that even his friend, Mr. Ryecross, would no longer pity him."

The judge dismissed the case, with a high compliment to Doctor Gambado, and with full costs to be paid into court by Mr. Deuce.

This action had some good effect upon this unhappy man, though it did not cure him of hypochondriacism. He rode out on horseback—on his new horse;—but whenever that horse came to the sign of the Red Cross, on Blackheath, directly opposite the four cross ways, he would lift up his nose, stand stockstill, and as if he would have his rider see the cross, and think upon it, he would not be persuaded to move. In vain did the lawyer tug at him, chuck his bridle, kick his sides, and use the most violent gesticulations to get him on. Whether he had a *nose* for the stables, or had been accustomed to Blackheath Red Cross on former days, he certainly had a nose, and until some one gently led him from the spot he would never be compelled to leave it. So he went by the name of *Old Deuce's Horse*, or, *The Horse with a Nose.*

> Hast thou a nose to smell a rat?
> Beware thou get not tit for tat.
> 'Tis better far to keep thy nose,
> Than have it split by angry foes.
> Avoiding strife, go, follow good,
> No harm will reach thee in such mood.

CHAPTER XV.

Me, my Wife, and Daughter.

WHO can look upon the comfortable enjoyment of good and happy people, in their latter days, and not delight to see them ?   Such a picture as this, drawn originally by Henry Banbury, Esq. and meant to convey a picture of domestic felicity in his day, would probably produce excessive ridicule if seen in these fast days.   If, now, such a sight were seen in Rotten-row, however pleasing to the philanthropist, it would be called an affectation of absurdity.   Yet Doctor Gambado, to the last year of his life, rode in such felicity that he was the only man in his profession that exactly practised the advice he gave.   A contrast to everything in the present day,—we say to everything like modern enjoyment.

One hundred years ago, there were no puffing steam engines, drawing thousands, with the rapidity of lightning, to Brighton, Ramsgate, Margate, and Folke-

R.C.   F. Bunbury Esq.

stone. Men all tell us, that domestic felicity is the same. We do not doubt it; but we find very few, very few, indeed, so blest with content, and so happy in their mutual society, as our respected friend, when, with his wife and daughter by his side, he rode a jog trot at the seaside, or the hillside, or along the fashionable road of life.

The Doctor had toiled through good report and evil report, and, like a prudent wise man, provided the best he could for his own. He kept up his house in Bread-street, though he declined practice altogether, that is, for *pecuniary profit*.

I question whether the Society for the Prevention of Cruelty to Animals would not have considered this an overloaded beast; but there was no such society in existence then. The weary camel, toiling over the waste, might be overloaded; but he would let his driver know how much he would carry. John Tattsall furnished his good friend, the Doctor, with elephantine horses, stout, stiff, strong, bony and sinewy; he was, without the aid of Doctor Cassock, the inventor of a wicker pannier of such ample dimensions, as to afford the most easy and convenient chair for each of the ladies, without exposing feet or ancles, or incommoding boots or dress. Now, indeed, ladies who travel in first-class carriages by rail, find the seats too narrow and almost destructive to their crinoline.

Hurrah for good people! Hurrah for happy people, wherever we can find them! Hurrah for the man who never allows his domestic felicity to be disturbed by any outward circumstances,—let his condition of life be among the highest or the lowest in the land! Hurrah for him who has the least ambition to gratify, except that of doing good to his neighbour! Hurrah for a grateful heart wherever it can be found! But whilst we thus laud the domestic comfort of real good people, let us not forget that they must have passed through many troubles and trials to gain that peace and serenity of mind, which our happy trio, Geoffery Gambado, his wife, and daughter, enjoyed. They had no affected display of superior accomplishments to delight society, and had no flattering encomiums passed upon them for their gentility. They were gentle, well informed, quiet, loveable people. They spoke that which they considered right, and always did the right thing as it ought to be done. The law which their good and excellent pastor taught them, they never departed from, viz. "That of doing to others, as they would others should do to them."

They kept the holiest law of true goodness, *Love one another*, in its perfect sense.

Doctor Gambado well knew who gave him a wife; and when he married, he resolved to perform the solemn vow he then made, and he kept his vow,—so did his wife her's,—and they were as happy a couple as could well be seen or known upon the face of the earth.

In his time, God's blessing was sought to enable him to keep his vow. There was no law then permitting men to go and be married without any asking of God's blessing upon such a step. Marriage was not then degraded into the unholy thing it is now, and conscience merely made to answer to a legal contract, which difference of opinion, or quarrels, or contrariety of disposition, may get dissolved in a divorce court. " For better for worse, for richer for poorer, till death us do part," is no longer the sole and solemn bond of matrimony. But the Doctor was a Christian in the noblest sense, and in domestic life his religion was his conscience, his wisdom, and his happiness. As little parade as man could make of outward profession was his study, but his heart was in the right place.

Where that is the case, ignorance and presumption, imposition and folly, are unknown. Men may ridicule simplicity of life and manners ; but there is an honesty of heart superior to all affectation, which need never be afraid.

The troubles of life are always borne well by those who observe the law of God ; and those who do not, never get any real release from them. They may get riches ; they may hide the blush of coveteousness ; but they have very little real comfort within themselves, because of the very changes which they themselves and all things around them undergo.

Doctor Gambado enjoyed every change of life, and lost no good condition either. He could look upon the calm sea with delight, and with the serenity of one who had not lived in vain. He always entertained the kindliest feelings of a brother for his sincere friend, Doctor Cassock, who used to drop in with any new number of the Spectator, and enjoy it. The domestic evenings spent in classical friendship are among the purest scholastic as well as domestic enjoyments.

Envy he had none, and therefore was most to be envied of those who, like Mr. Deuce, or anyone else, never enjoyed the happiness of another. Promote the welfare of another, and you will find your own comfort increased. Detract from another, and nothing but envy will be your increase.

The object with which this book was begun, and is finished, is to let you see, reader, how to make something out of that which might to many appear worse than nothing.

Suppose that sixteen drawings of this character were given you, with nothing but the heading of each chapter written under them,—would you have made out a more comprehensive description of the probability of their truth? There is some profit in the labour, if your heart is in any way cheered by beholding the ingenuity of man. Works of art, or works of great expense, or great works of any kind, the Author makes no kind of pretence to perform; yet, if you are pleased with his ingenuity, grudge not a helping hand at any time to reward industry.

> Ah! little thought Gambado, in his day,
> As on he passed through life's uneven way,
> How many toils and troubles he would scan,
> Before he reached the common age of man!
> Yet on he went; and as his years declined,
> And quietude and peace becalmed his mind,
> He felt and owned, no greater bliss could be
> Than resignation for Eternity.
> "Ah!" he would say, "behold, dear wife, you sea,
> ' Each wave seems striving for celebrity!
> ' It rolls along until it reach the shore,
> ' Then bursts in froth,—and then is seen no more!
> ' Still, on and on succeeding waves advance,
> ' And thus perpetual motion would enhance.
> ' 'Tis so with mortals striving on and on,
> ' They reach the shore,—and all their toil is gone.
> ' How oft yon waves, by angry tempests tost,
> ' Like human passions, are in fury lost;
> ' Dash'd on the rocks, their crested pride, in foam
> ' Sprays into atoms ere it finds a home.

' So mighty strugglers after this world's fame,
' Find all their fury perish with their name.
' 'Tis seldom known that speculators thrive,
' Or long their great inventions may outlive.
' Others come on,—no end of new things known,
' One age will praise,—the next, the praise disown.
' Feathers you wear,—but feathers blown away,
' Will be succeeded by some new display.
' We ride on horseback, and survey the tide,—
' The age will come, that horses none will ride ;
' The age will be that coaches will no more
' Be seen with horses, two, or three, or four ;
' But on will pass, and leave no other trace,
' Than iron's friction from a rapid pace."

What would Gambado think, if he could see
His own predictions made a verity ?
Who can predict one single year's advance ?
Truth is so strange it seems a day's romance.
Things that last year were mighty,—are all gone ;
Works of great hope,—are perished and undone.
Iron is moulded by the human hand ;
And wooden walls no more the seas command.
All would be great, be rich, and all invent,
But few there are, who are at all content.
With lightning speed intelligence conveyed
From land to land, the iron rails are laid,—
And 'neath the ocean's deep united cords,
Convey the merchant's or the prince's words.
But mostly all, by sea, or land, or train,
Is that the traffickers may get their gain.

The greatest gain, that ever man could get,
Is sweet contentment after every fret.
When projects are completed, all is vain,
For other projects follow in their train;
Old age comes on,—all projects quickly cease,—
Happy are they who live and die in peace.
Gambado did so: Reader, may thy fame
Rest with content on One Blest, Holy Name!

THE END.

www.ingramcontent.com/pod-product-compliance
Lightning Source LLC
Chambersburg PA
CBHW030601270326
41927CB00007B/1003